Beware the Cat

BEWARE THE CAT

By William Baldwin

The First English Novel

Introduction and Text
by

WILLIAM A. RINGLER, JR.

and

MICHAEL FLACHMANN

1988

HUNTINGTON LIBRARY
SAN MARINO, CALIFORNIA

Library of Congress Cataloging-in-Publication Data

Baldwin, William, ca. 1518-1563?
  Beware the Cat: the first English novel / by William Baldwin :
introduction and text by William A. Ringler, Jr. and Michael
Flachmann.

  p. cm.
  Bibliography: p.
  1. Cats—Fiction. 2. Satire, English. 3. Fiction—Translations from for-
eign languages—History and criticism. 4. English Fiction—Early
modern, 1500-1700—History and criticism. I. Ringler, William A.,
1912-1987. II. Flachmann, Michael. III. Title.
PR2209.B15B4   1988   823'.3—dc19   88-13057
                                                         CIP
Published 1988.
First paperback edition 1995.
Printed in the United States of America.

This edition printed with the support of
the Betty Leigh Merrell Memorial Fund

ISBN 0-87328-087-3
ISBN 0-87328-154-3 pbk.

For Evelyn

CONTENTS

PREFACE

MY attention was first called to William Baldwin's *Beware the Cat* by Arundel Esdaile's listing of it in his bibliography *English Tales and Prose Romances to 1740* (1912) and by Friedrich Brie's long essay and summary entitled "William Baldwin's *Beware the Cat*" in *Anglia*, 37 (1913): 303-350. My interest was in narrative, and after an extended study of the entire earlier tradition of English prose fiction, I reached the conclusion that *Beware the Cat* was the first original work of prose fiction of more than short-story length in English, the first English "novel" if you will, and in terms of artistic merit one of the two or three very best examples of sixteenth-century English fiction.

For several years I assigned the text in a graduate seminar in early fictional narrative at the University of Chicago, with uniformly enthusiastic reactions from the students. Then my friend Steven W. May called to my attention British Library MS Additional 24,628, a careful transcript of the now-lost 1570 first edition of the printed text, which is more complete and more accurate than the 1584 edition which served as the copy text for the only modern reprint of *Beware the Cat*, a limited-issue old-spelling edition published by William P. Holden in 1963. So I decided that a new edition—complete with a modernized text based on this recently discovered manuscript, expanded annotations, and an essay detailing the beginnings of the English novel—would help restore *Beware the Cat* to its rightful place in the history of English prose fiction.

I wish to thank the Trustees of the British Library, who gave me permission to modernize the text of MS Additional 24,628 and to quote other texts in their collections, and also the authorities of the Bodleian, University of Chicago, Folger, and Huntington Libraries for the use of various items in their collections. G.E. Bentley searched the Bagford Papers for me for traces of the 1652 edition; A.T. Brissenden provided me with information about the folk-tale dissemination of the "Grimalkin is dead" story; Patrick Collinson checked my account of the Reformation; John C. MacGregor IV helped with botanical identifications; and Paul M. Zall read through my modernization of Baldwin's text and clarified more than one puzzling passage. I am also grateful to the editors of *Novel* for permission to reprint materials originally published in "*Beware the Cat* and the Beginnings of

English Fiction'' (12 [1979]: 113-126). My final debt of gratitude is to Michael Flachmann, who has worked steadily with me on this manuscript since he was a doctoral student at Chicago in 1969; he helped transcribe the text from the original manuscripts, provided many of the annotations, and collaborated with me in the preparation of the introduction.

William A. Ringler, Jr.

ADDENDUM

Professor William Ringler did not live to see this edition of *Beware the Cat* in print. He died suddenly on the afternoon of 1 January 1987 while working in his study at home in Pasadena. Fortunately he had examined and approved the final typescript of the book prior to his death, though he had not seen either the galleys or page-proofs. This last stage of preparing the manuscript for publication has of necessity been left to me and to Guilland Sutherland, scholarly publications editor at the Huntington Library. I am also indebted to James Thorpe and Robert Middlekauff, both former directors of the Huntington Library who have been continuously supportive of this project; to Virginia Renner and the staff of the Readers' Services department of the Library; to Jane Evans, past editor of the Huntington Press; and to Stanley Stewart, James Riddell, John Steadman, and Elizabeth and Dan Donno for their helpful advice on various matters of style and content. Finally, I am grateful for the loving encouragement offered by Bill's wife, Evelyn, to whom this book is dedicated, and by his daughter Susan, who is herself a scholar. During his lifetime, William Ringler was a kind, modest man whose great erudition, perseverance, and generosity of spirit marked him as a pre-eminent scholar and teacher. Although all of us who knew him are deeply saddened by his death, we are glad that his edition of *Beware the Cat* can now be added to the rich legacy of literary scholarship he left behind.

Michael Flachmann

INTRODUCTION

THE long fictional narrative in prose, what is now called the "novel," has been the dominant literary form in the west since the eighteenth century, although it was the latest to be developed in most literatures of the world. To study the art of narrative in earlier times, we must examine works composed in verse—especially the epic and the romance—because the history of earlier literatures confirms that the more highly organized rhythms of verse invariably preceded the looser rhythms of prose. This is not to say that primitive peoples did not tell one another stories in prose, but rather that they ordinarily did not elaborate them and record them in that medium (except for short anecdotes, such as the fables attributed to Aesop or the story told by Herodotus of the clever thief who deceived Rhampsinitus). Since verse is more easily memorized than prose, an oral society could more accurately hand down longer works if they were structured metrically. And even after the invention of writing, at first only literary works in verse were considered of sufficient dignity to merit the labor of being recorded.

Prose fiction itself came late to England, with original prose fiction later still. Not until the second third of the sixteenth century did England produce an original work of prose fiction of more than short-story length (see the appendix of this book for a history of English prose narratives written prior to 1558). All the preceding longer works had been translations, or at best adaptations, of narratives originally written in French, Latin, German, Dutch, or Greek. The earliest work that approaches being original fiction is Sir Thomas Elyot's *Image of Governance* (1541), a compilation of the "acts and sentences notable" of the Roman Emperor Alexander Severus. Sir Thomas boasted that his work was history, a translation of an ancient Greek manuscript, but the contents were partly compiled and partly invented by Elyot himself. Though his work is semi-fictional, it contains scant narrative. Rather than providing an account of the events of the emperor's reign, Elyot merely furnishes a collection of letters and speeches illustrating points of public policy.

Another partly original work of fiction is the popular *Scoggin's Jests*, written by Andrew Borde prior to 1549. This is a compilation of seventy-eight short anecdotes, ranging in length from two or three sentences to two or three pages; many of the stories were drawn from identifiable sources, while others were taken from oral tradition or invented by Borde himself. The jest books, the earliest and best of which was *A Hundred Merry Tales* (1525), were collections of detached jokes and humorous brief narratives.[1] In *Scoggin's Jests*, Borde attempted to give unity and coherence to a variety of anecdotes by attaching them to a fictional character, the Oxford scholar and wandering jester Tom Scoggin, who eventually entered the service of the king of England and later the king of France.

These detached anecdotes of the late medieval jest books, when collected under the name of a single character such as Til Eulenspiegel, Virgilius, or the Parson of Kalenberg, become the forerunners of the picaresque novel and other pseudo-biographical works of fiction. But original English examples of this genre featuring a single, unified narrative did not appear until much later, in the 1590s, which saw publication of the anonymous *Long Meg of Westminster* and the popular stories of London artisans and merchants written by Thomas Deloney. Although he took some of his episodes from the jest books, Deloney attached them to more completely realized characters in a clearly drawn social setting and structured them according to a more definite plot line. In contrast, Borde's Scoggin is not consistently delineated (he is sometimes a scheming confidence man, while at other times he plays tricks for fun); although he is made a participant in each episode, the incidents are seldom linked together in a logical sequence of action. Until William Baldwin's *Beware the Cat*, written in the first half of 1553, we can find no original work of English fiction of more than short-story length in which we see consistent character portrayal and a sequence of events that form a coherent plot.

William Baldwin

Baldwin has established a permanent place in the annals of English literature as the editor and main author of the verse narratives collected in *A Mirror for Magistrates* (1559). His contribution to the history of prose fiction, however, has been strangely ignored.[2] In fact, no history of the novel, from John C. Dunlop in 1814 to Paul Salzman in 1985, pays any attention to Baldwin. This neglect deserves remedy, because *Beware the Cat* is not only the first original work of longer prose fiction in English, but it is also of considerable artistic excellence—which makes it more interesting and more entertaining than most of the prose works in English immediately following it.

William Baldwin—who was in turn a poet, printer, prose writer, and preacher—was of Welsh descent, though the identity of his parents and the date and place of his birth are unknown.[3] A "William Baulden" supplicated for the B.A. at Oxford in January of 1532/3, yet no record exists of his admission to the degree.[4] Whether this is a form of the name "Baldwin," and if so whether this William was our author, is uncertain because the name, which appears in a variety of spellings, was quite common during the sixteenth century. His later publications show him to be an educated man, though he could have acquired his learning through a combination of grammar school and private study, rather than through attending a university. The earliest confirmed biographical information we have concerning Baldwin is that he was an assistant to the publisher Edward Whitchurch from 1547 until 1553. Whitchurch was a London merchant who, because of his commitment to the Protestant Reformation, became a publisher and with Richard Grafton issued the earliest editions of the English Bible. About 1545, Whitchurch bought what had been Wynkyn de Worde's printing house at the Sun in Fleet Street, and from then until the accession of the Roman Catholic Queen Mary in July 1553 he published sixty-eight books—mainly Bibles, primers, editions of the metrical versions of the Psalms, the first and second Prayer Books of Edward VI, other religious works, and the writings of his "servant" William Baldwin. Like his employer, Baldwin was clearly a dedicated supporter of the Protestant Reformation and a violent opponent of Roman Catholicism.

Baldwin's first known publication, which appeared in April of 1547/8, was a commendatory sonnet (the first English sonnet to appear in print) prefixed to Christopher Langton's treatise entitled *The Principal Parts of Physic*, which was printed by Whitchurch. In January 1547/8 he published *A Treatise of Moral Philosophy* in four books, also printed by Whitchurch, which he dedicated to the eight-year-old son of Protector Somerset. Baldwin's most popular book, this Tudor compendium of ancient philosophy went through twenty-five editions by 1651.[5]

In June 1549 he issued *The Canticles or Ballads of Solomon in English Meters*, "Imprinted at London by William Baldwin servaunt with Edward Whitchurche," which he dedicated to the eleven-year-old King Edward VI. Three years later, he translated from Latin the libellous *Wonderful News*

of the Death of Paul the Third, in which the supposed satirical author,
P. Esquillus (Pasquil), pretends to follow the soul of the late pope to hell
where his crimes are engraved on pillars of adamant.[6] In accordance with
conventional Protestant interpretation, the Church of Rome is identified
with the scarlet woman who rode upon the seven-headed beast in Revela-
tion 17, and Pope Paul III is accused of murder, incest, bribery, and oppression of Lutherans. That Baldwin chose to translate this work shows the
virulence of his anti-papal feelings. From it he learned the effectiveness of
first-person narrative as a vehicle for religious satire.

Judging from his dedication of the *Treatise of Moral Philosophy* to the
son of the Protector and the *Canticles of Solomon* to the king himself,
Baldwin appears to have hoped for employment at court. But such an
appointment was not immediately forthcoming, because four months later
Somerset fell from power and was eventually executed. Finally, during the
Christmas season of 1552/3, Baldwin was asked to work at court as an actor,
deviser of entertainments, and provider of stage properties under the Master
of the King's Pastimes, George Ferrers. The Revels Accounts for December
through June of this period record his activities.[7] In a letter written in early
December 1552, Ferrers specified that he needed a "divine," an
"astronomer," and others in his train—a statement that agrees with the
Argument of *Beware the Cat*, which explains that Streamer and Willot were
Ferrers' "divine" and "astronomer." On 27 December, Ferrers requested
"Irish apparel for a man and a woman," while subsequent accounts for
January and February record properties for a "Mask of Cats" and "An Irish
Play of the State of Ireland" by Baldwin to be presented before the king.
Because of the king's illness, the mask and play were postponed from 2
February until 2 April; they may, in fact, never have been performed at
all, since young Edward died on 6 July and, after the brief reign of
the unfortunate Queen Jane, Queen Mary ascended the throne, overthrew
the Reformation, and restored Roman Catholicism as England's national
religion. During this time of political and religious turmoil in the early
months of 1553, Baldwin composed his most important work of prose fiction, *Beware the Cat*, in which cats are principal actors and the early scenes
are set in Ireland.

Since *Beware the Cat* is not only a fictional narrative but also a religious
satire, some knowledge of the religious controversies of the time is necessary for readers to appreciate it fully. Luther had posted his theses at Wit-
tenberg in 1517, and as a result Protestant doctrine spread rapidly through

the German states, Switzerland, France, the northern Netherlands, and England. Though in 1534 Henry VIII broke administratively with the Church of Rome and proclaimed himself "supreme head in earth of the Church of England," he remained outwardly a conservative in theology; consequently, only minor changes occurred in doctrine or liturgical observances during his reign (except for the publication of one English translation of the Bible). When the boy king Edward VI ascended the throne early in 1547, the Protector Somerset took over rule of the kingdom and favored the Protestants; later, under Northumberland, the more radical reformers were allowed full sway. Such an abrupt shift in religious sympathies is nowhere more evident than in the fate of Dr. Richard Smith, the Regius Professor of Divinity at Cambridge, who in 1546 had published *The Assertion and Defense of the Sacraments of the Altar*—a defense, dedicated to King Henry VIII, of current Roman Catholic doctrine. In the early months of the reign of Henry's son, Smith also published *A Treatise Setting Forth Diverse Truths Necessary to be Believed Which Are Not Expressed in the Scripture but Left to the Church by the Apostles' Tradition*, for which he was immediately clapped into prison and forced to make public recantation of the ideas set forth in both books. During the rest of Edward's short reign, only Protestant tracts were allowed into print. Somerset had clearly established freedom of the press—but for Reformers only.

The main attacks levied by Protestants against the Church of Rome concerned what they considered to be the superstitious accretions imposed by Rome upon primitive (and therefore supposedly "pure") Christian observances: that is, articles of belief and ritual not found in the text of the Bible but handed down through the "traditions" of the Church. Reformers criticized the veneration of saints, the issuance of indulgences, the celibacy of the clergy, the conducting of church services in Latin rather than in the vernacular, the celebration of the Mass itself (especially the attribution of any immediately practical efficacy), and, in the later part of Edward's reign, the doctrine of transubstantiation, which alleged the real presence of the body and blood of Christ in the Holy Eucharist.

Attacks on the Mass reached their height in 1548, when the English printing presses poured forth thirty-two editions of twenty-three tracts and pamphlets against it. Early in 1549, Parliament approved the provisions of the first Prayer Book of Edward VI and ordered them in full force by Whit Sunday (the ninth of June). These required the destruction of images and the abolition of all observances and articles of belief based solely on "tradition." The Latin Mass was abolished, and an English Communion Service was substituted in which the laity were allowed to receive communion in both kinds and in which the bread and wine were considered merely symbolic rather than real. Whitchurch printed his first edition of the *Book of Common Prayer* on 7 March 1549 and the revised version in the spring or early summer of 1552.

This background against which *Beware the Cat* was written is reflected in episode after episode ridiculing the many Catholic observances objected to by the Protestants—observances which, they asserted, stemmed from superstition and belief in magic. The numbers game played in the two accounts of the death of Grimalkin, for example, suggests the fantastic grounds upon which oral reports came to be credited and accepted as "unwritten verities": in the first tale, a man had met a cat in Kankwood forty years ago who told him that Grimalkin was dead; and in the second, an Irish churl had reported to Thomas thirty-three years ago that Patrick Apore had had an adventure seven years prior to that in which he killed the fiend-like cat he met in the church. This satire of oral tradition is made even more obvious in Thomas' account of how witches hand down the secrets of their magic from mother to daughter, for Baldwin adds the marginal note, "Witchcraft is kin to unwritten verities, for both go by traditions." Similarly, belief in the physical efficacy of the Mass is undermined by the story of the supposedly blind country woman who was cured by a sight of the sacramental wafer, while the adoration of images is mocked in the story of the old bawd who says her beads before a statue of the Virgin.

In the early months of 1553 young Edward VI became seriously ill, and it became obvious that he would soon be succeeded by his sister, the Roman Catholic Mary. Baldwin's employer Whitchurch was—with John Day, Richard Grafton, and William Seres—among the most prominent publishers of Protestant service books and anti-Catholic propaganda. In order to safeguard his financial assets, he deeded in June the contents of his printing house to the stationers William and Humphrey Powell, and the following October entered a writ of recovery against them through an intermediary.[8] By this legal maneuver, Whitchurch was able to go into hiding and at the same time recover some of the capital of his business. His fears were prophetic, for on the accession of Queen Mary he was specifically excepted from the general pardon that she issued, and his friends Day and Seres were imprisoned.

Upon the death of Edward, Baldwin composed a long poem, *The Funerals of King Edward the Sixth*, which he did not dare publish until 1560, two years after the accession of Queen Elizabeth. Meanwhile, the operation of Whitchurch's shop was taken over by the scrivener John Wayland, who was granted, on 24 October 1553 (three months after the accession of Queen Mary), an exclusive patent for printing Roman Catholic primers—two weeks before Parliament had decided on the restoration of the old form. Baldwin apparently kept his religious opinions to himself, and he continued his employment in the same shop under Wayland, who in 1556 printed an updated sixth edition of Baldwin's *Treatise of Moral Philosophy*, which was intended to counter Paulfreyman's pirated edition then in circulation. Since copy for the new primer was not received until spring of 1555 (Wayland's first edition was dated June 4th), to keep his press and staff occupied Wayland prepared an edition of John Lydgate's *Fall of Princes*, adding to it a continuation prepared by Baldwin and others entitled *A Memorial of Such Princes, as Since the Time of King Richard the Second, Have Been Unfortunate in the Realm of England*. This edition was in print by September 1554 but was soon afterwards suppressed by the government (only a two-leaf fragment survives); it was not printed again until 1559 when, under Queen Elizabeth, it was newly titled *A Mirror for Magistrates*. The suppressed edition probably contained twenty-one "tragedies" of unfortunate Englishmen, ranging from Robert Tresilian (who died in 1388) to Edward IV (who died in 1483). Baldwin's friend George Ferrers provided four of these verse histories, Thomas Chaloner one, and Thomas Phaer another; a poem of earlier composition about Edward IV was attributed, no doubt wrongly, to John Skelton; and Baldwin himself may have composed most of the remaining fourteen poems. The 1559 *Mirror* contained only nineteen tragedies, though its table of contents listed twenty-one. Another edition in 1563 added eight more tragedies, two of which were by Baldwin, who had planned the new volume and had written the prose links between different sections. Eight editions of the *Memorial* or *Mirror* appeared between 1554 and 1609, making it one of the most influential collections of poems in Elizabeth's reign. Many other poems were modeled on Baldwin's *Mirror*, which was also important in shaping English history plays and English conceptions of dramatic tragedy.[9]

Queen Mary at first proceeded slowly and temperately with her restoration of Roman Catholicism. In February of 1554, however, Sir Thomas Wyatt (son of the poet) raised a rebellion in protest against her proposed marriage to Philip II of Spain. The government struck back swiftly, condemning

Wyatt and forty-three of his followers to be hanged, drawn, and quartered, with their mutilated bodies set up on every gate of London as a warning to future traitors. In April, an unknown person hanged on the gallows in Cheapside a cat suited like a Mass priest with a shaven crown and a round piece of paper between its forefeet to represent the communion wafer.[10] In February of the next year, the first Marian martyr, John Rogers, was burned at the stake; thereafter the fires flamed regularly in Smithfield and other parts of the country, until by the end of Mary's reign more than three hundred Protestants had been burned or had died in prison, while over eight hundred had fled the realm.

Despite his Protestant sympathies, Baldwin continued offering his plays for performance at the court of Queen Mary. In December of 1556, for example, he wrote to the Master of the Revels presenting him "a Comedie concerning the way to Lyfe, mete. . .to be played before the quene."[11] It featured sixty-two characters, each of whose names began with the letter "L," and would have taken three hours to perform. No evidence exists that his offer was accepted.

After the accession of Queen Elizabeth, Baldwin was "called to another trade of life" in January 1560 when he was ordained deacon; soon thereafter he undoubtedly became a priest when he was appointed vicar of Tortington in Sussex and later, in 1561, rector of St. Michael le Quern in Cheapside. He also continued his interest in publishing during this time, for in 1563 the London publisher Thomas Marsh engaged him to assist the antiquary John Stow in preparing an abridgment of English chronicles to supersede Grafton's. The end of Baldwin's life was near, however. During the latter half of 1563 the plague raged in London, and more than seventeen thousand people died—perhaps twenty per cent of the city's population. In September the Marian Roman Catholic bishops were removed from the Tower, where they had been imprisoned for protection from the plague, and put under house arrest in the country by the bishops who had succeeded them. In the same breath, Stow reported both the fate of the bishops and the demise of William Baldwin: "Their deliverance, or rather change of prison, did so much offend the people that the preachers at Paul's Cross and in other places. . .preached, as it was thought of many wise men very seditiously, as Baldwin at Paul's Cross, wishing a gallows set up in Smithfield and the old bishops and other papists hanged thereon. Himself died of the plague the next week after."[12]

Baldwin's Narrative Art

Though Baldwin does not appear from Stow's report to have been a kindly man, he was an unusually competent writer—more competent in prose than in verse. His principal prose work, *Beware the Cat*, first published seven years after his death, is not only the first original piece of long prose fiction in English, but it is also one of the best and most interesting works of its kind produced in the sixteenth century. Longer examples of English fiction before Baldwin were all translations or adaptations. As the first original writer in his field, Baldwin apparently borrowed little from his immediate predecessors. We can locate a few literary precedents, however. Thomas More, who led his readers to accept the marvels of Utopia by his matter-of-fact account of meeting the traveler Raphael Hythloday in the garden of his friend Peter Giles in Antwerp, may have provided a hint for Baldwin's circumstantial opening scene in the chamber of Master Ferrers on the 28th of December 1552. John Clerc's translation of Diego de San Pedro's *Arnalte y Lucenda* (1542) may have suggested the device of the first-person narrator who, in attempting to build himself up, unwittingly tears himself down. Similarly, Baldwin's own translation of *Wonderful News of the Death of Paul the Third* may have reminded him of the effectiveness of first-person narrative in religious satire. Caxton's translation of the Dutch *Reynard the Fox* (1481), a satirical story in which animals act like people, would seem to be a natural precursor to *Beware the Cat*; in contrast, however, Baldwin's cats act like cats—articulate felines possessing terrifying supernatural powers of evil. The components of a few of the episodes in Baldwin's story are borrowed. His tale of the Irish werewolf, for example, is from a manuscript of Giraldus Cambrensis' *Topographia Hiberniae*, his presciential pills from *Tales and Quick Answers*, and his old bawd and weeping cat from Caxton's *Fables of Aesop*. But Baldwin invented the main elements of his story himself, gave it a vivid setting in his own place and time, devised complicated and interesting ways of telling it, greatly advanced the art of characterization, and made his fiction a vehicle for important ideas.

The earlier romances had been set in unidentified, far-away places in times long past. But Baldwin blended enough sober fact with his outrageous fiction to provide a pretense of verisimilitude. Some of his characters were living persons: the prominent courtier George Ferrers, who was Master of the King's Pastimes during the 1552-53 Christmas season; Richard Sherry,

who published two books in 1550; the Irish rebel Cahir Mac Art, who died
in 1554; and Baldwin himself. Even the names "Streamer" and "Willot"
appear obscurely in contemporary records. Furthermore, the action of *Beware
the Cat* takes place at a definitely specified time in locations that are clearly
described and recognizable.

The time of the action is, for Baldwin's readers, the immediate past.
Streamer delivers his oration, "turning himself so in his bed as we might
best hear him," in Master Ferrers' lodging at court on the 28th of December
1552. Streamer mixed his potion "about solstitium estivale" (that is, June
11, Old Style). Mouse-slayer reports the main events of the last two years
of her life, beginning with her residence at Stratford "in the time when
preachers had leave to speak against the Mass, but it [the Mass] was not
forbidden till half a year after" (that is, during the first half of 1549) and
continuing until she clawed the gallant behind the arras "at Whitsuntide
last," two years later (which would be 17 May 1551). Therefore, Streamer
mixed his potion and heard the cats speak at the end of spring in 1551,
a year and a half before he reported his adventure to Baldwin and Ferrers.
As a result, the main events of his narration clearly reflect the climate of
opinion prevailing in England after June 1549 when the Latin Mass was
abolished and the services in the new English *Book of Common Prayer* were
made compulsory. A similar concern for chronology and accuracy of local
detail is shown in the account of the death of Grimalkin.

The house where Streamer hears tales about Ireland, concocts his potion,
and listens to the cats—the printing house above Aldersgate—is more specifically located than any place in earlier English literature. "More roomish
within than garish without," it is set accurately in London: in the city wall
at the end of St. Martin's Lane, next to St. Anne's Church, where the bells
of St. Botolph's Bishopsgate could be heard a mile away. Baldwin has clearly
visualized his printing-house setting as an actual place, one that would have
been immediately recognizable to his sixteenth-century London readers as
the premises of the well-known Reformation printer John Day.

Streamer's chamber is also clearly delineated and precisely oriented:
located at the end of the printing house, over the kitchen, with a "fair bay
window opening into the garden, the earth whereof is almost as high as
Saint Anne's Church top, which standeth thereby," and through which the
moon could be seen above the steeple of Mile End Church. The room has
another trellis window which looks down upon the leads of Aldersgate, where
"sometime quarters of men, which is a loathly and abhominable sight, do

stand upon poles." The room also has a fireplace large enough to stand in. Many of Baldwin's other descriptions are equally authentic. Thus the Irish kern Patrick Apore wore "a corslet of mail made like a shirt" and a helmet of "gilt leather...crested with otter skin"; to cook their meat, he and his boy, "after their country fashion...did cut a piece of the hide and pricked it upon four stakes which they set about the fire, and therein they sod a piece of the cow," a description borne out by the woodcut portraying an Irish feast in John Derricke's *Image of Ireland* (1581), used on the jacket of this book.

Most of the earlier works of English fiction had been simple linear narratives told in the third person by two-dimensional narrators; the main emphasis was on situation and action, and the characters were only slightly developed. In contrast, Baldwin tells his story in the first person, though he speaks in his own person only at the beginning and end of the narrative. In the central portion, he reports what Master Streamer had told him about his own experiences; Streamer, while telling his own first-person story, narrates in turn stories told to him by four other people gathered at the house of John Day; and finally, Streamer repeats a cat's autobiographical narrative that he has overheard.

In addition to the complicated maneuvering of different points of view, in which the narrative is structured like inter-nesting boxes, Baldwin's characterization is quite extraordinary—especially that of Streamer, the principal narrator. Chaucer had said that

> Whoso shall tell a tale after a man,
> He mote rehearse as nigh as ever he can
> Everich a word (*Canterbury Tales*, A, 731-733).

Similarly, Baldwin explains that he has "so nearly used both the order and words of him that spake them (which is not the least virtue of a reporter) that I doubt not but [the readers]...shall in the reading think they hear Master Streamer speak, and he himself in the like action shall doubt whether he speaketh or readeth." As a result, Baldwin has Streamer characterize himself by the rhythm of his clauses and by his unique, pompous style. Streamer begins his oration with a Mistress Quickly-like performance of complete recall and free association, but in his attempt to impress his listeners he unconsciously reveals himself as a pedantic fool. He spews forth Latin quotations and esoteric bits of learning that are often ludicrously incorrect. He pretends to be adept in all sciences and solemnly asserts that the astronomers are wrong in supposing that the changes of the moon cause the variation of the tides; on the contrary, he claims that the tides cause the changes of the moon—his own Copernican hypothesis, though he had never heard of Copernicus. He is a coiner of bizarre terms, such as "like-nightical" for "equinoctial," and he delights in a virtuoso parade of rhyming terms in enumerating the "barking of dogs, grunting of hogs, wawling of cats, rumbling of rats," etc. He praises his friend Thomas by saying that no others could have done so well, "except myself, and a few more of the best learned alive."

In addition to allowing Streamer to reveal himself unwittingly in his speech, Baldwin also uses a device of characterization not available to present-day authors: this is the marginal note, by means of which he can, while maintaining his pose of impartial reporter, comment amusingly or satirically upon the action. For example, when Streamer reports that the moon "saw me neither in my bed nor at my book," Baldwin writes acidly in the margin, "The man is studious." When Streamer launches into rhymed prose on the "wawling of cats, rumbling of rats," Baldwin observes in the margin, "Here the poetical fury came upon him." And when Streamer speaks of himself "and a few more of the best learned alive," Baldwin adds this marginal note: "The best learned are not the greatest boasters."

Baldwin also uses marginalia to guide the responses of his readers by explaining significances they may have overlooked. Thus when Streamer, adopting an air of great learning, discourses on the astrological importance of planetary hours, but confuses them with solar hours, Baldwin notes in the margin, "Master Streamer varieth from the astronomers in his planetary hours." Similarly, when the old bawd tells the merchant's wife that the weeping cat is her daughter, Baldwin adds, "A shameful lie shamefully set forth." The author also frequently points up the satirical and theological application of references and episodes by marginal comment. In response to Streamer's use of the term "Popish conjurer," for instance, Baldwin observes gravely, "Transubstantiationers destroy Christ's manhood."

So, in *Beware the Cat* we have a fantastic fiction set realistically in the London of Baldwin's own time; a very original handling of point of view—a first-person narrative with authorial comment; an enveloping action; and satirical characterization, in which the narrator by his speech produces an effect quite the opposite of that which he intends. Baldwin also presents us with a novel of ideas—ideas of pressing contemporary importance reflecting the religious struggles of the Protestant Reformation. In *Beware the Cat*, the author is playing a very complex fictional game: he uses an illusion to destroy what he considers to be an illusion. The general thrust of his fictional argument is that only a person gullible enough to believe a character as outrageous as Gregory Streamer would believe in the "unwritten verities" handed down by the "traditions" of the Church. In literature, contrary to what one expects in other disciplines, more complex productions are sometimes created before more simple ones. This is certainly the case in the history of English prose fiction, for Baldwin's narrative techniques were more sophisticated than those of most writers of fiction before the nineteenth century.

After *Beware the Cat*, the next original work of English fiction is the pseudonymous Oliver Oldwanton's *Image of Idleness* (ca. 1555), a series of letters purportedly between Bawdin Bachelor and Walter Wedlock, which can be called the first English epistolary novel. This was followed in about 1567 by the jest-book biography *Merry Tales by Master Skelton*. Then came Gascoigne's *Adventures of Master F.J.* (1573). About 1576, Thomas Whythorne completed *A Book of Songs and Sonnets with Discourses of the Child's, Young Man's and Entering Old Man's Life*, which remained in manuscript until 1961, when it was edited by James M. Osborn as *The Autobiography of Thomas Whythorne*. This is a first-person narrative which ostensibly recounts the events of the first forty-seven years of the author's life. The main function of the narrative, however, is to frame and provide occasion for 197 poems, which makes it a work similar in kind to Gascoigne's prose and verse *Adventures of Master F.J.* and his verse *Dan Bartholomew of Bath*; in fictional technique, the narrative is like Gabriel Harvey's *A Noble Man's Suit to a Country Maid*, which recounts the attempted seduction of the author's otherwise unknown sister, Mercy, in the later months of 1574.

In 1577 appeared John Grange's *The Golden Aphrodite*, a pedantically humorous mythological tale of courtship with more attention to style than to action. The following year John Lyly's amazingly popular *Euphues the Anatomy of Wit* was published, a collection of "euphuistic" speeches and letters strung upon the thinnest possible thread of narrative. In 1579, Stephen Gosson's *Ephemerides of Phialo* was printed, a fictional refutation of Lyly's *Euphues* (but unfortunately couched in a similar style).

In 1580, no fewer than seven original works of prose fiction were brought to completion: Nicholas Breton's *Miseries of Mavillia* (in his *Will of Wit*), the episodic autobiography of a female Lazarillo de Tormes; W.C.'s *Adventures of Lady Egeria*, a formless amalgam of perjury, murder, matricide, infanticide, adultery, and incestuous rape—every kind of horror and perversion that could be invented—set forth in a pretentiously inflated style; Robert Greene's *Mamillia, a Looking Glass for the Ladies of England*, an imitation of Lyly that marked Greene's debut as a prolific novelist; Lyly's *Euphues and his England*, a sequel to his earlier popular success; Anthony Munday's *Zelauto the Fountain of Fame Erected in an Orchard of Amorous Adventures*, another imitation of *Euphues* but with a stronger narrative line; Austin Saker's *Narbonus the Labyrinth of Liberty*, yet another Euphuistic imitation; and finally, and best of all, the first version of Philip Sidney's *The Countess of Pembroke's Arcadia*. This last work was begun in 1577 and completed in 1580, but remained in manuscript until 1926. It is a tragi-comedy, blending the chivalric and pastoral in a five-act dramatic structure. Four years later, Sidney undertook a radical revision and expansion of the work, which he then began *in medias res*, and rewrote the action in an enormously complex, interlaced fashion. He broke off in what was probably the middle of his revision, and this incomplete version was printed in 1590. It continued to be the most highly admired work of English fiction for more than a hundred years.

If we set aside Elyot's *Image of Governance* as being not even minimally narrative and *Scoggin's Jests* as lacking an adequate story line, then *Beware the Cat* remains as the first original English work of prose fiction of more than short-story length. It is also, in terms of artistry and interest, one of the very best productions of sixteenth-century European fiction and compares well with the much-admired Spanish *La vida de Lazarillo de Tormes*, with which it shares many characteristics and which was printed only a year after the composition of Baldwin's work. *Beware the Cat* cannot equal in artistic merit the unfortunately incomplete revised version of Sidney's *Arcadia* (1590), which is by any measure the best piece of sixteenth-century prose fiction produced in any language, but it does stand on a par with or ahead of other now highly regarded works of early English fiction by Nashe, Gascoigne, Lodge, and Deloney.

NOTES

1. Most of the early jest books have been edited by W.C. Hazlitt, *Shakespeare Jest-Books* (3 vols., London, 1864), and Paul M. Zall, *A Hundred Merry Tales and Other English Jest-books* (Lincoln, Nebraska, 1963).

2. In 1912, Arundel Esdaile listed *Beware the Cat* in his standard bibliography, *A List of English Tales and Prose Romances Printed Before 1740*; and the following year, Friedrich Brie published a long article on it in *Anglia* (37:303-350), arguing that it was the "erste originelle prosdaerzählung" in English (but his article was not listed in the first *Cambridge Bibliography of English Literature* [1940] and so dropped from sight). In 1963, the late William P. Holden reprinted the text of the inferior 1584 edition, but in his introduction he discussed it only as satire and made no mention of it as original fiction.

3. In the prose introduction to the tragedy of Owen Glendower in the suppressed [1554] edition of *A Mirror for Magistrates* (ed. L.B. Campbell [Cambridge, 1938], opposite p. 8), Baldwin said that Owen Glendower was "a man of that country whence (as the Welshmen bear me in hand [i.e., inform me]) my pedigree is descended." The *Dictionary of National Biography* account is inadequate; there are better biographies by W.F. Trench, *Modern Quarterly of Language and Literature*, 1 (1899): 259-267, and E.I. Feasey, *Modern Language Review*, 20 (1925): 407-418. Authorities for facts not mentioned by either Trench or Feasey are here noted.

4. C.W. Boase, *Register of the University of Oxford*, 1 (1885): 173.

5. Whitchurch printed three more editions in the early 1550s. About 1555, Richard Tottel issued a fifth edition "newelye sette foorthe and enlarged by Thomas Paulfreyman." This omitted Baldwin's name from the title page, substituted a new dedication by Paulfreyman to Lord Henry Hastings, omitted most of Baldwin's first book, and slightly expanded and rearranged the remaining contents in seven books. About 1556, Baldwin reissued his original four-book version, "Newly perused and augmented by W.B. first author thereof," in which he objected "to have any other man plowe with my oxen, or to alter or augmente my doynges." Nevertheless, the following year Tottel reprinted Paulfreyman's seven-book version unchanged. In the last year of his life, Baldwin made a final attempt to regain some control over the work he had originally composed, apparently entering into an agreement with Tottel to issue another edition of his own work partly in its original form but also accepting some of the revisions introduced by Paulfreyman. This appeared posthumously in 1564—expanded to ten books. Notwithstanding, in 1567 Tottel issued what was in actuality a ninth edition of the *Treatise* in twelve books, "Fyrst gathered and set foorthe by Wylliam Baudwin, and nowe once againe augmented, and the third tyme enlarged by Thomas Paulfreyman." This third revision by Paulfreyman was reprinted sixteen times between 1571 and 1651 without essential change. Baldwin finally did receive part credit on the title page as co-author; but his dedication and prologue were usurped by Paulfreyman's, and though much of the wording of the book remained his, its organization was greatly changed. Baldwin similarly suffered

from later augmentations and revisions by others of his *Mirror for Magistrates*. His publishing career illustrates how difficult it was for a Tudor author to retain control of his own text.

6. This has not heretofore been attributed to Baldwin, but his authorship is established by the combination of his initials, "W.B., Londoner," on the title page, and his personal motto "Love and Live" (which he appended to all of his works) in the preface.

7. Albert Feuillerat, *Documents Relating to the Revels at Court in the Time of King Edward VI and Queen Mary* (Louvain, 1914), 89-125.

8. Henry R. Plomer, "An Inventory of Wynkyn de Worde's House 'The Sun in Fleet Street' in 1553," *The Library*, 3rd series, 6 (1915): 228-229 and 234.

9. See Willard Farnham, *The Medieval Heritage of Elizabethan Tragedy* (Berkeley, 1936), chaps. 8-10.

10. Charles Wriothesley, *A Chronicle of England*, ed. W.D. Hamilton, *Camden Society*, new series 11, Part 2 (1877): 114, Robert Crowley's continuation of Thomas Lanquet, *An Epitome of Chronicles*, 1559, 4F4.

11. Friedrich Brie, "William Baldwin als Dramatiker," *Anglia*, 38 (1914): 157-172. Historians of the drama have mistakenly cited the title as "Love and Live," which is not a title but Baldwin's motto.

12. James Gairdner, ed., "Historical Memoranda in the Handwriting of John Stowe, from Lambeth MS 306," in *Three Fifteenth-Century Chronicles, Camden Society*, new series 28 (1880): 126; and also Brit. Lib. MS Harley 367, f.3, printed by Charles L. Kingsford, *A Survey of London by John Stow*, 1 (Oxford, 1908): ix-x, xlviii-xlix.

In July 1569 Roger Ireland was licensed to print "beware the Catt by Wylliam Bawdw[i]n" (Arber, *Transcript*, 1 [1875]: 389). Joseph Ritson (*Bibliographia Poetica*, 1802, 118) is the only authority for an edition dated 1561, which is probably an error. A record of a fourth edition, printed and published by Jane Bell in 1652, was reported by W.C. Hazlitt (*Hand-Book*, 1867, 23) to be among the sixty-four volumes of the Bagford papers in the British Library, but it cannot now be found. The Northern Rebellion in the latter part of 1569 and the pope's excommunication of Queen Elizabeth early the following year made anti-Catholic satire attractive. Roger Ireland apparently assigned his rights, and there were three sixteenth-century editions.

[70] Printed by John Allde for John Arnold, 1570. No copy extant, but known from A.

[A] British Library MS Additional 24,628. A careful transcript, made in 1847, from a printed copy of 70 which had been in the possession of B.H. Bright but cannot now be located. In 1864 J.O. Halliwell[-Phillipps] published an edition of ten copies printed from an incompetent transcript of A, which omitted all the side-notes and introduced numerous verbal errors on every page.

[G] STC 1244, printed and published by Wylliam Gryffith, 1570. Survives only in a fragment consisting of the first four leaves (British Library C60.b.8); reprinted by Holden, pp. 90-93.

[84] STC 1245, printed by Edward Allde (son of John) in 1584. Copies, both lacking title pages, are in the British Library (Huth 66) and Folger Shakespeare Library; a single leaf (A4) is in the Bodleian (Douce fragment f.45). The Folger copy was reprinted by William P. Holden in 1963 (Connecticut College Monograph No. 8) with correction of only twelve obvious misprints.

When we compare the four-leaf fragment of G with A and 84, we find twenty-four verbal variants. In this segment, the text of A appears to be perfect except for a single-word error; G is apparently in error in 16 passages (of which 5 are omissions); and 84 is apparently in error in 6 of these (of which 2 are omissions). It is therefore clear that the three extant texts are each in their turn direct copes of lost 70, that A is a remarkably accurate copy of 70, that G is a careless copy of 70, and that 84 is a moderately careful copy of 70. Therefore A is the primary textual authority, on which this edition is based, and its readings have been preferred before those of G and 84 except in cases of demonstrable error.

Since all three of the substantive texts stand at least at a third remove from Baldwin's lost holograph original, we cannot expect the accidentals of spelling, capitalization, and even punctuation to preserve Baldwin's own usages, because sixteenth-century compositors regularly edited their copy manuscripts by substituting their own patterns of accidentals for those of the originals. Therefore, we have punctuated the text in a way to make it intelligible to modern readers and have normalized the spelling in conformity to present-day usage. In the notes that follow the text of the novel, we list G and 84 variants only when we have preferred them to A or when we have found emendation necessary.

A MARVELOVS

Hystory intituled, Beware the
Cat. Conteynyng diuerse wounder-
full and incredible matters.
Uery pleasant and mery to read.

❀

¶ IMPRINTED AT LONDON, IN
Fleetestrete at the signe of the
Faulcon by *Wylliam Gryffith:*
and are to be sold at his shop
in S. Dunstons Church=
yarde. Anno. 1570.

T.K. to the Reader

[1584]

This little book, *Beware the Cat*,
    most pleasantly compiled,
In time obscured was, and so
    since that hath been exiled.

[5]

Exiled because, perchance at first,
    it showed the toys and drifts
Of such as then, by wiles and wills,
    maintained Popish shifts.

[10]

Shifts such as those, in such a time,
    delighted for to use,
Whereby full many simple souls
    they did full sore abuse.

[15]

Abuse? Yea sure, and that with spight,
    whenas the Cat gan tell
Of many pranks of Popish priests
    both foolish, mad, and fell.

[20]

Fell? Sure, and vain, if judgment right
    appear to be in place,
And so as fell in pleasant wise
    this fiction shows their grace.

[25]

Grace? Nay sure, ungraciousness
    of such and many mo,
Which may be told in these our days
    to make us laugh also.

Also to laugh? Nay, rather weep
  to see such shifts now used,
And that in every sort of men
  true virtue is abused.

[5]

Abused? Yea, and quite down cast,
  let us be sure of that;
And therefore now, as hath been said,
  I say, "Beware the Cat."

[10]

The Cat full pleasantly will show
  some sleights that now are wrought,
And make some laugh which unto mirth
  to be constrained are loath.

[15]

Loath? Yea, for over-passing grief
  that much bereaves their mind,
For such disorder as in states
  of every sort they find.

[20]

Find? Yea, who can now boast but that
  the Cat will him disclose?
Therefore, in midst of mirth I say,
  "Beware the Cat" to those.

[25]

Vale.

THE EPISTLE DEDICATORY

Love and Live.
To the Right Worshipful Esquire
Master John Young,
Grace and Health.

I have penned for your mastership's pleasure one of
the stories which Master Streamer told the last
Christmas, and which you so fain would have heard
reported by Master Ferrers himself. And although I
be unable to pen or speak it so pleasantly as he could,   [5]
yet have I so nearly used both the order and words
of him that spake them (which is not the least virtue
of a reporter) that I doubt not but that he and Master
Willot shall in the reading think they hear Master
Streamer speak, and he himself in the like action shall   [10]
doubt whether he speaketh or readeth. I have divided
his oration into three parts, and set the argument
before them and an instruction after them, with such
notes as might be gathered thereof, so making it book-
like, and entitled *Beware the Cat.*   [15]
But because I doubt whether Master Streamer will
be contented that other men plow with his oxen (I
mean pen such things as he speaketh, which perhaps
he would rather do himself to have, as he deserveth,
the glory of both), therefore I beseech you to learn his   [20]
mind herein, and if he agree it pass in such sort, yet
that he peruse it before the printing and amend it if
in any point I have mistaken him. I pray you likewise
to ask Master Ferrers his judgement herein, and show
him that the *Cure of the Great Plague*, of Master   [25]
Streamer's translation out of the Arabic which he sent
me from Margate, shall be imprinted as soon as I may
conveniently.
And if I shall perceive by your trial that Master
Streamer allow my endeavors in this kind, I will here-   [30]
after, as Plato did by Socrates, pen out such things of
the rest of our Christmas communications as shall be

to his great glory, and no less pleasure to all them that desire such kinds of knowledge. In the meanwhile I beseech you to accept my good will, and learn to Beware the Cat. So shall you not only perform that

[5]　　I seek, but also please the Almighty, who always preserve you. Amen.

Yours to his power,
G[ulielmus] B[aldwin].

THE ARGUMENT

It chanced that at Christmas last I was at Court with
Master Ferrers, then master of the King's Majesty's
pastimes, about setting forth of certain interludes,
which for the King's recreation we had devised and
were in learning. In which time, among many other   [5]
exercises among ourselves, we used nightly at our
lodging to talk of sundry things for the furtherance
of such offices wherein each man as then served. For
which purpose it pleased Master Ferrers to make me
his bedfellow, and upon a pallet cast upon the rushes   [10]
in his own chamber to lodge Master Willot and Master
Streamer, the one his Astronomer, the other his
Divine. And among many other things too long to
rehearse, it happened on a night (which I think was
the twenty-eight of December), after that Master   [15]
Ferrers was come from the Court and in bed, there
fell a controversy between Master Streamer, who with
Master Willot had already slept his first sleep, and me,
that was newly come unto bed, the effect whereof was
whether birds and beasts had reason.   [20]
    The occasion thereof was this: I had heard that the
King's players were learning a play of Aesop's Crow
wherein the most part of the actors were birds, the
device whereof I discommended, saying it was not
comical to make either speechless things to speak or   [25]
brutish things to common reasonably; and although
in a tale it were sufferable to imagine and tell of some-
thing by them spoken or reasonably done (which kind
Aesop laudably used), yet it was uncomely, said I, and
without example of any author, to bring them in lively   [30]
personages to speak, do, reason, and allege authorities out of authors. Master Streamer, my lord's

5

Divine, being more divine in this point than I was ware of, held the contrary part, affirming that beasts and fowls had reason, and that as much as men, yea, and in some points more.

[5] Master Ferrers himself and his Astronomer wakened with our talk and harkened to us, but would take part on neither side. And when Master Streamer had for proof of his assertion declared many things (of elephants that walked upon cords, hedgehogs that

[10] knew always what weather would come, foxes and dogs that after they had been all night abroad killing geese and sheep would come home in the morning and put their necks into their collars, parrots that bewailed their keepers' deaths, swallows that with celandine open

[15] their young ones' eyes, and an hundred things more), which I denied to come of reason, and to be but natural kindly actions, alleging for my proof authority of most grave and learned philosophers.

"Well," quoth Master Streamer, "I know what I

[20] know, and I speak not only what by hearsay of some philosophers I know, but what I myself have proved."

"Why," quoth I then, "have you proof of beasts' and fowls' reason?"

"Yea," quoth he, "I have heard them and under-

[25] stand them both speak and reason as well as I hear and understand you."

At this Master Ferrers laughed. But I, remembering what I had read in Albertus' works, thought there might be somewhat more than I did know; wherefore

[30] I asked him what beasts or fowls he had heard, and where and when. At this he paused awhile, and at last said: "If that I thought you could be content to hear me, and without any interruption till I have done mark what I say, I would tell you such a story of one piece

[35] of mine own experimenting as should both make you wonder and put you out of doubt concerning this matter; but this I promise you afore, if I do tell it, that as soon as any man curiously interrupteth me, I

will leave off and not speak one word more.'' When we had promised quietly to hear, he, turning himself so in his bed as we might best hear him, said as followeth.

THE FIRST PART OF
MASTER STREAMER'S ORATION

Being lodged (as, I thank him, I have been often) at
a friend's house of mine, which, more roomish within
than garish without, standeth at Saint Martin's Lane
end and hangeth partly upon the town wall that is
called Aldersgate (either of one Aldrich, or else of
Elders, that is to say ancient men of the city which
among them builded it—as bishops did Bishopsgate;
or else of eldern trees, which perchance as they do in
the gardens now thereabout, so while the common
there was vacant grew abundantly in the same place
where the gate was after builded, and called thereof
Elderngate—as Moorgate took the name of the field
without it, which hath been a very moor; or else,
because it is the most ancient gate of the City, was
thereof in respect of the other, as Newgate, called the
Eldergate; or else, as Ludgate taketh the name of Lud
who builded it—so most part of heralds, I know, will
soonest assent that Aluredus builded this; but they
are deceived, for he and his wife Algay builded Aldgate, which thereof taketh the name as Cripplegate
doth of a cripple, who begged so much in his life, as
put to the silver weather cock which he stole from
Paul's steeple, after his death builded it). But where-
ofsoever this gate Aldersgate took the name (which
longeth chiefly to historiers to know), at my friend's
house, which, as I said, standeth so near that it is over
it, I lay oftentimes, and that for sundry causes, sometime for lack of other lodging, and sometime as while
my Greek alphabets were in printing to see that it
might truly be corrected. And sure it is a shame for
all young men that they be no more studious in the
tongues; but the world is now come to that pass, that

*Why Aldersgate
was so named.
Bishops builded
Bishopsgate.*

[10]

Why Moorgate.

*Why Newgate.
Why Ludgate.*

*Why Aldgate.
Why Cripplegate.*

*Paul's weather-
cock was silver.*

[25]

*Against young
men's negligence.*

9

if he can prate a little Latin and handle a racquet and
a pair of six-square bowls, he shall sooner obtain any
living than the best learned in a whole city; which is
the cause that learning is so despised and baggagical
things so much advanced.

While I lay at the foresaid house for the causes afore-
said, I was lodged in a chamber hard by the Printing
House, which had a fair bay window opening into the
garden, the earth whereof is almost as high as Saint

Anne's Church top, which standeth thereby. At the
other end of the Printing House, as you enter in, is
a side door and three or four steps which go up to the
leads of the Gate, whereas sometime quarters of men,
which is a loathely and abominable sight, do stand

up upon poles. I call it abominable because it is not
only against nature but against Scripture; for God com-

manded by Moses that, after the sun went down, all
such as were hanged or otherwise put to death should
be buried, lest if the sun saw them the next day His

wrath should come upon them and plague them, as
He hath done this and many other realms for the like
transgression. And I marvel where men have learned
it or for what cause they do it, except it be to feed
and please the devils. For sure I believe that some

Evil spirits live
by the savor of
man's blood.

spirits, Misanthropi or Molochitus, who lived by the
savor of man's blood, did, after their sacrifices failed
(in which men were slain and offered unto them), put
into butcherly heathen tyrants' heads to mangle and
boil Christian transgressors and to set up their quarters

for them to feed upon. And therefore I would counsel
all men to bury or burn all executed bodies, and
refrain from making such abominable sacrifice as I
have often seen, with ravens or rather devils feeding
upon them, in this foresaid leads—in the which every

night many cats assembled, and there made such a
noise that I could not sleep for them.

Wherefore, on a time as I was sitting by the fire with
certain of the house, I told them what a noise and what

a wawling the cats had made there the night before
from ten o'clock till one, so that neither I could sleep
nor study for them; and by means of this introduction we fell in communication of cats. And some
affirming, as I do now (but I was against it then), that
they had understanding, for confirmation whereof one
of the servants told this story.

"There was in my country," quod he, "a man" (the
fellow was born in Staffordshire) "that had a young
cat which he had brought up of a kitling, and would
nightly dally and play with it; and on a time as he
rode through Kankwood about certain business, a cat,
as he thought, leaped out of a bush before him and
called him twice or thrice by his name. But because
he made none answer nor spake (for he was so afraid
that he could not), she spake to him plainly twice or
thrice these words following: 'Commend me unto
Titton Tatton and to Puss thy Catton, and tell her that
Grimalkin is dead.' This done she went her way, and
the man went forward about his business. And after
that he was returned home, in an evening sitting by
the fire with his wife and his household, he told of
his adventure in the wood. And when he had told
them all the cat's message, his cat, which had harkened
unto the tale, looked upon him sadly, and at the last
said, 'And is Grimalkin dead? Then farewell dame,'
and therewith went her way and was never seen after."

When this tale was done, another of the company,
which had been in Ireland, asked this fellow when this
thing which he had told happened. He answered that
he could not tell well, howbeit, as he conjectured, not
passing forty years, for his mother knew both the man
and the woman which ought the cat that the message
was sent unto. "Sure," quod the other, "then it may
well be; for about that same time, as I heard, a like
thing happened in Ireland where, if I conjecture not
amiss, Grimalkin of whom you spake was slain."

"Yea sir," quod I, "I pray you how so?"

A wise man may in some things change his opinion.

[10]

A cat spake to a man in Kankwood.
[15]

[20]

A wonderful wit of a cat.

[30]

[35]
Grimalkin was slain in Ireland.

"I will tell you, Master Streamer," quod he, "that
which was told me in Ireland, and which I have till
now so little credited, that I was ashamed to report
it. But hearing that I hear now, and calling to mind
my own experience when it was, I do so little misdoubt
it that I think I never told, nor you ever heard, a more
likely tale. While I was in Ireland, in the time that
Mac Murrough and all the rest of the wild lords were
the King's enemies, what time also mortal war was
between the Fitz Harrises and the Prior and Convent
of the Abbey of Tintern, who counted them the King's
friends and subjects, whose neighbor was Cahir Mac
Art, a wild Irishman then the King's enemy and one
which daily made inroads into the county of Wexford
and burned such towns and carried away all such cattle
as he might come by, by means whereof all the country
from Clonmines to Ross became a waste wilderness and
is scarce recovered until this day. In this time, I say,
as I was on a night at coshery with one of Fitz Harris'
churls, we fell in talk (as we have done now) of strange
adventures, and of cats. And there, among other
things, the churl (for so they call all farmers and hus-
bandmen) told me as you shall hear.

"There was, not seven years past, a kern of John
Butler's dwelling in the fassock of Bantry called Patrick
Apore, who minding to make a prey in the night upon
Cahir Mac Art, his master's enemy, got him with his
boy (for so they call their horse-keepers be they never
so old knaves) into his country, and in the night time
entered into a town of two houses, and brake in and
slew the people, and then took such cattle as they
found, which was a cow and a sheep, and departed
therewith homeward. But doubting they should be
pursued (the cur dogs made such a shrill barking), he
got him into a church, thinking to lurk there till midnight was past, for there he was sure that no man
would suspect or seek him—for the wild Irishmen have
had churches in such reverence (till our men taught

*Experience is
an infallible
persuader.*

*Civil war between
the King's
subjects.*

*The fashion of
the Irish wars.*

[20]

A churl's tale.
[25]

[30]
*This was an
Irish town.*

*Irish curs
bark sore.*

them the contrary) that they neither would, nor durst, either rob ought thence or hurt any man that took the churchyard for sanctuary, no, though he had killed his father.

The wild Irishmen were better than we in reverencing their religion.
[5]

"And while this kern was in the church he thought it best to dine, for he had eaten little that day. Wherefore he made his boy go gather sticks, and strake fire with his feres, and made a fire in the church, and killed the sheep, and after the Irish fashion laid it thereupon and roasted it. But when it was ready, and that he thought to eat it, there came in a cat and set her by him, and said in Irish, 'Shane foel,' which is, 'give me some meat.' He, amazed at this, gave her the quarter that was in his hand, which immediately she did eat up, and asked more till she had consumed all the sheep; and, like a cormorant not satisfied therewith, asked still for more. Wherefore they supposed it were the Devil, and therefore thinking it wisdom to please him, killed the cow which they had stolen, and when they had flayed it gave the cat a quarter, which she immediately devoured. Then they gave her two other quarters; and in the meanwhile, after their country fashion, they did cut a piece of the hide and pricked it upon four stakes which they set about the fire, and therein they sod a piece of the cow for themselves, and with the rest of the hide they made each of them laps to wear about their feet like brogues, both to keep their feet from hurt all the next day, and also to serve for meat the next night, if they could get none other, by broiling them upon coals.

The old Irish diet was to dine at night.
[10]

A malapert guest that cometh unbidden.
[15]
A cat eat a sheep.

[20]

The woodkern's cookery.

"By this time the cat had eaten three quarters and called for more. Wherefore they gave her that which was a-seething; and doubting lest, when she had eaten that, she would eat them too because they had no more for her, they got them out of the church and the kern took his horse and away he rode as fast as he could hie. When he was a mile or two from the church the moon began to shine, and his boy espied

Kerns for lack of meat eat their shoes roasted.

[35]

the cat upon his master's horse behind him and told
him. Whereupon the kern took his dart, and turning
his face toward her, flang it and struck her through
with it. But immediately there came to her such a sight

*A kern killed
Grimalkin.*
[5]
of cats that, after long fight with them, his boy was
killed and eaten up, and he himself, as good and as
swift as his horse was, had much to do to scape.

*Cats did kill and
eat a man.*

"When he was come home and had put off his har-
ness (which was a corslet of mail made like a shirt, and

The kern's armor.
[10]
his skull covered over with gilt leather and crested with
otter skin), all weary and hungry he set him down by
his wife and told her his adventure, which, when a
kitling which his wife kept, scarce half a year old, had
heard, up she started and said, 'Hast thou killed Gri-

[15]
malkin!' And therewith she plunged in his face, and
with her teeth took him by the throat, and ere that
she could be plucked away, she had strangled him.
This the churl told me now about thirty-three winters

*A kitling killeth
the kern that
slew Grimalkin.*
[20]
past; and it was done, as he and divers other creditable
men informed me, not seven years before. Whereupon
I gather that this Grimalkin was it which the cat in
Kankwood sent news of unto the cat which we heard

*A very strange
conjecture.*
of even now."

"Tush," quod another that sat by, "your conjecture

[25]
is too unreasonable; for to admit that cats have reason
and that they do in their own language understand
one another, yet how should a cat in Kankwood know
what is done in Ireland?"

"How?" quod he, "even as we know what is done

*Each realm
knoweth what is
done in all other.*
in the realms of France, Flanders, and Spain, yea, and
almost in all the world beside. There be few ships but
have cats belonging unto them, which bring news unto

Cats carry news.
their fellows out of all quarters."

"Yea," quod the other, "but why should all cats

[35]
love to hear of Grimalkin, or how should Grimalkin
eat so much meat as you speak of, or why should all
cats so labor to revenge her death?"

"Nay, that passeth my cunning," quod he, "to show

in all; howbeit in part conjectures may be made, as thus. It may be that Grimalkin and her line is as much esteemed and hath the same dignity among cats, as either the humble or master bee hath among the whole hive, at whose commandment all bees are obedient, whose succor and safeguard they seek, whose wrongs they all revenge; or as the Pope hath had ere this over all Christendom, in whose cause all his clergy would not only scratch and bite, but kill and burn to powder (though they knew not why) whomsoever they thought to think but once against him—which Pope, all things considered, devoureth more at every meal than Grimalkin did at her last supper."

"Nay," said I then, "although the Pope, by exactions and other baggagical trumpery, have spoiled all people of mighty spoils, yet (as touching his own person) he eateth and weareth as little as any other man, though peradventure more sumptuous and costly, and in greater abundance provided. And I heard a very proper saying in this behalf of King Henry VII: When a servant of his told him what abundance of meat he had seen at an abbot's table, he reported him to be a great glutton; he asked if the abbot eat up all, and when he answered no, but his guests did eat the most part, 'Ah,' quod the king, 'thou callest him glutton for his liberality to feed thee and such other unthankful churls.' Like to this fellow are all ruffians, for let honest, worshipful men of the city make them good cheer or lend them money as they commonly do, and what have they for their labor? Either foul, reproachful names (as 'dunghill churls,' 'cuckold knaves'), or else spiteful and slanderous reports, as to be usurers and decayers of the common weal. And although that some of them be such indeed, yet I abhor to hear other of whom they deserve well, so lewdly to report them. But now, to return to your communication, I marvel how Grimalkin (as you term her), if she were no bigger, could eat so much meat at once."

Bees love and obey their governor.

The Pope's clergy are crueller than cats.
The Pope a great waster.

[15]
A little sufficeth him that hath enough.

[20]

Such jests a man may have enough.

The wisdom of King Henry the Seventh.
[30]

[35]
The unthankful are to be abhorred.

"I do not think," quod he that told the tale, "that she did eat all (although she asked all), but took her choice and laid the rest by, as we see in the feeding of many things. For a wolf, although a cony be more than he can eat, yet will he kill a cow or twain for his breakfast—likewise all other ravenous beasts. Now, that love and fellowship and a desire to save their kind is among cats, I know by experience. For there was one that hired a friend of mine, in pastime, to roast a cat alive, and promised him for his labor twenty shillings. My friend, to be sure, caused a cooper to fasten him into a hogshead, in which he turned a spit, whereupon was a quick cat. But ere he had turned a while, whether it was the smell of the cat's wool that singed, or else her cry that called them, I cannot tell, but there came such a sort of cats that if I and other hardy men (which were well scrat for our labor) had not behaved us the better, the hogshead, as fast as it was hooped, could not have kept my cousin from them."

"Indeed," quod a well-learned man and one of excellent judgment that was then in the company, "it doth appear that there is in cats, as in all other kinds of beasts, a certain reason and language whereby they understand one another. But, as touching this, Grimalkin I take rather to be an hagat or a witch than a cat. For witches have gone often in that likeness—and thereof hath come the proverb, as true as common, that a cat hath nine lives (that is to say, a witch may take on her a cat's body nine times)."

"By my faith, sir, this is strange," quod I myself, "that a witch should take on her a cat's body. I have read that the Pythonesses could cause their spirits to take upon them dead men's bodies, and the airy spirits which we call demons (of which kind are incubus and succubus, Robin Goodfellow the fairy, and goblins, which the miners call telchines) could at their pleasure take upon them any other sorts. But that a woman, being so large a body, should strain her into the body

[5]
Ravenours spoil more than they occupy. Like loveth the like.

A quick cat roasted.

[15]
Cat will to kind.

Some think this was Master Sherry.

Witches may take upon them the likeness of other things.

[30]

Airy spirits take on them dead men's bodies.
[35]

of a cat (or into that form either), I have not much heard of, nor can well perceive how it may be, which maketh me (I promise you) believe it the less.''

''Well, Master Streamer,'' quod he, ''I know you are not so ignorant herein as you make yourself; but this is your accustomed fashion, always to make men believe that you be not so well learned as you be. *Sapiens enim celat scientiam*, which appeared well by Socrates. For I know, being skilled as you be in the tongues (chiefly the Calde, Arabic, and Egyptian) and having read so many authors therein, you must needs be skillful in these matters; but where you spake of instrusion of a woman's body into a cat's, you either play Nichodem or the stubborn Popish conjurer: whereof one would creep into his mother's belly again, the other would bring Christ out of Heaven to thrust him into a piece of bread (but as the one of them is gross and the other perverse, so in this point I must place you with one of them). For although witches may take upon them cats' bodies, or alter the shape of their or other bodies, yet this is not done by putting their own bodies thereinto, but either by bringing their souls for the time out of their bodies and putting them in the other, or by deluding the sight and fantasies of the seers. As when I make a candle with the brain of a horse and brimstone, the light of the candle maketh all kinds of heads appear horseheads, but yet it altereth the form of no head, but deceiveth the right conception of the eye (which, through the false light, receiveth a like form).''

Then quod he that had been in Ireland, ''I cannot tell, sir, by what means witches do change their own likeness and the shapes of other things, but I have heard of so many and seen so much myself, that I am sure they do it. For in Ireland, as they have been ere this in England, witches are for fear had in high reverence. They be so cunning that they can change the shapes of things as they list at their pleasure and

Wise men dissemble their cunning.

Master Streamer is well seen in tongues.

[15]
Transubstantia-tioners destroy Christ's manhood.

[20]

How witches transform their shape.
[25]

One kind of magic consisteth in deceiving the senses.

Witches are reverenced for fear.

so deceive the people thereby that an act was made in Ireland that no man should buy any red swine. The cause whereof was this: The witches used to send to the markets many red swine, fair and fat to see unto as any might be, and would in that form continue long; but if it chanced the buyers of them to bring them to any water, immediately they found them returned either into wisps of hay, straw, old rotten boards, or such like trumpery, by means whereof they lost their money or such other cattle as they gave in exchange for them.

An act forbidding to buy red swine.

Sorcerers make swine of hay and other baggage.

"There is also, in Ireland, one nation whereof some one man and woman are at every seven years' end turned into wolves, and so continue in the woods the space of seven years. And if they hap to live out the time, they return to their own form again, and other twain are turned for the like time into the same shape—which is a penance (as they say) enjoined that stock by Saint Patrick for some wickedness of their ancestors. And that this is true witnessed a man whom I left alive in Ireland who had performed this seven years' penance, whose wife was slain while she was a wolf in her last year. This man told to many men, whose cattle he had worried and whose bodies he had assailed while he was a wolf, so plain and evident tokens and showed such scars of wounds which other men had given him, both in his man's shape before he was a wolf and in his wolf's shape since, which all appeared upon his skin, that it was evident to all men (yea, and to the bishop, too, upon whose grant it was recorded and registered) that the matter was undoubtedly past all peradventure.

Men turned into wolves.

Saint Patrick's plague.

A man proved himself to have been a wolf seven years.

A Bishop confirmeth Saint Patrick's plague.

[35]

"And I am sure you are not ignorant of the hermit whom, as St. Augustine writeth, a witch would in an ass's form ride upon to market. But now how these witches made their swine, and how these folk were turned from shape to shape, whether by some ointment whose clearness deceived men's sights till either the water washed away the ointment, or else that the clearness of the water excelled the clearness of the ointment (and so betrayed the operation of it), I am as uncertain as I am sure that it were the spirits called demons, forced by enchantments, which moved those bodies till shame of their shape discovered caused them to leave them. But as for the transformation of the wolves, [it] is either miraculous as Naaman's leprosy in the stock of Gehesie, or else [due] to shameful, crafty, malicious sorcery. And as the one way is unsearchable, so I think there might means be found to guess how it is done the other way. For witches are by nature exceeding malicious, and if it chance that some witch, for displeasure taken with this wolvish nation, gave her daughter charge in her death bed when she taught her the science (for till that time witches never teach it, nor then but to their eldest and best-beloved daughter) that she should, at every seven years' end, confect some ointment which seven years' space might be in force against all other clearness to represent unto men's eyes the shape of a wolf; and in the night season to go herself in likeness either of the mare or some other night form and anoint therewith the bodies of some couple of that kindred which she hated; and that after her time she should charge her daughter to observe the same, and to charge her daughter after her to do the like forever, so that this charge is given always by tradition with the science, and so is continued and observed by this witch's offspring, by whom two of this kindred (as it may be supposed) are every seven years' space turned into wolves.''

When I had heard these tales and the reason of the doing showed by the teller, ''Ah, Thomas,'' quod I (for that was his name; he died afterwards of a disease which he took in Newgate, where he lay long for suspicion of magic because he had desired a prisoner to promise him his soul after he was hanged), ''I perceive now the old proverb is true: 'The still sow

How sorcerers may make swine.

Demons are the souls of counterfeit bodies.

[10]

Witches are by nature malicious.
[15]
When and to whom witches teach their science.
How men are changed into wolves.

[25]
Witchcraft is kin to unwritten verities, for both go by traditions.
[30]

[35]
Many shrewd diseases do breed in Newgate.

*The best learned
are not the
greatest boasters.*
[5]

*That a man
seeth, he may
boldly say.*

*A woman was
found in a cat's
likeness and
punished.*

*Witches never
use their art but
to evil.*

[25]
*It is to be
thought that
Grimalkin was
a witch.*
[30]
*Cats may be
deceived as well
as Christian folk.*

[35]

eateth up all the draff.' You go and behave yourself
so simply that a man would think you were but a fool,
but you have uttered such proof of natural knowledge
in this your brief talk, as I think (except myself and
few more the best-learned alive) none could have done
the like.''

"You say your pleasure, Master Streamer," quod he.
"As for me, I have said nothing but that I have seen,
and whereof any man might conjecture as I do.''

"You have spoken full well," quod he that gave
occasion of this tale, "and your conjectures are right
reasonable. For like as by ointments (as you suppose)
the Irish witches do make the form of swine and wolves
appear to all men's sight, so think I that by the like
power English witches and Irish witches may and do
turn themselves into cats. For I heard it told while I
was in the university, by a credible clerk of Oxford,
how that in the days when he was a child an old
woman was brought before the official and accused for
a witch, which (in the likeness of a cat) would go into
her neighbors' houses and steal thence what she listed.
Which complaint was proved true by a place of the
woman's skin, which her accusers (with a firebrand that
they hurled at her) had singed while she went a-
thieving in her cat's likeness. So that, to conclude as
I began, I think that the cat which you call Grimalkin,
whose name carrieth in it matter to confirm my conjecture (for Malkin is a woman's name, as witnesseth
the proverb 'there be more maids than Malkin'), I
think, I say, that it was a witch in a cat's likeness; and
that for the wit and craft of her, other natural cats that
were not so wise have had her and her race in reverence
among them, thinking her to be but a mere cat as they
themselves were—like as we silly fools long time, for
his sly and crafty juggling, reverenced the Pope,
thinking him to have been but a man (though much
holier than we ourselves were), whereas indeed he was
a very incarnated devil, like as this Grimalkin was an

incarnate witch."

"Why then, sir," said I, "do you think that natural cats have wit and that they understand one another?" "What else, Master Streamer?" quod he. "There is no kind of sensible creatures but have reason and understanding; whereby, in their kind, each understandeth other and do therein in some points so excel that the consideration thereof moved Pythagoras (as you know) to believe and affirm that after death men's souls went into beasts and beasts' souls into men, and every one according to his desert in his former body. And although his opinion be fond and false, yet that which drew him thereto is evident and true—and that is the wit and reason of diverse beasts, and again the dull, beastly, brutish ignorance of diverse men.

"But that beasts understand one another, and fowls likewise, beside that we see by daily experience in marking them, the story of the Bishop of Alexandria by record doth prove. For he found the means, either through diligence so to mark them, or else through magic natural so to subtiliate his sensible powers, either by purging his brain by dry drinks and fumes, or else to augment the brains of his power perceptible by other natural medicines, that he understood all kind of creatures by their voices. For being on a time sitting at dinner in a house among his friends, he harkened diligently to a sparrow that came fleeing and chirping to other that were about the house, and smiled to himself to hear her. And when one of the company desired to know why he smiled, he said 'At the sparrow's tale. For she telleth them,' quod he, 'that in the highway, not a quarter of a mile hence, a sack of wheat is even now fallen off a horseback and broken, and all the wheat run out, and therefore biddeth them come thither to dinner.' And when the guests, musing hereat, sent to prove the truth, they found it even so as he had told them."

All sensible creatures have reason and understanding.

Pythagoras' opinion concerning souls.

Some beasts are wiser than men.

A Bishop understood all kind of creatures' voices.

The brain is the organ of understanding.

A sparrow called her fellows to a banquet.

[35]

When this tale was ended, the clock struck nine;
whereupon old Thomas, because he had far to his
lodging, took his leave and departed. The rest of the
company got them also either to their business or to
their beds. And I went straight to my chamber (before
remembered) and took a book in my hand to have
studied, but the remembrance of this former talk so
troubled me that I could think of nothing else, but
mused still and, as it were, examined more narrowly
what every man had spoken.

*Master Streamer
is always given
much to study.*

[10]

THE SECOND PART OF
MASTER STREAMER'S ORATION

Ere I had been long in this contemplation, the cats, whose crying the night before had been occasion of all that which I have told you, were assembled again in the leads which I spake of, where the dead men's quarters were set up; and after the same sort as they did the night before, one sang in one tune, another in another, even such another service as my Lord's chapel upon the scaffold sang before the King. They observed no musical chords, neither diatesseron, diapente, nor diapason; and yet I ween I lie, for one cat, groaning as a bear doth when dogs be let slip to him, trolled out so low and so loud a bass that, in comparison of another cat which, crying like a young child, squealed out the shrieking treble, it might be well counted a double diapason. Wherefore, to the intent I might perceive the better the cause of their assembly, and by their gestures perceive part of their meaning, I went softly and fair into a chamber which hath a window into the same leads, and in the dark standing closely, I viewed through the trellis, as well as I could, all their gestures and behavior.

And I promise you it was a thing worth the marking to see what countenances, what becks, yea and what order was among them. For one cat, which was a mighty big one, grey-haired, bristle-bearded, and having broad eyes which shone and sparkled like two stars, sat in the midst, and on either side of her sat another. And before her stood three more, whereof one mewed continually, save when the great cat groaned. And ever when the great cat had done, this mewing cat began again, first stretching out her neck and, as it were, making 'beisance to them which sat.

Cats assembled in the leads.

Cats have sundry voices.

The diligence of the author to understand all things.

[20]

Cats keep order among themselves.

Cats make courtesy with their necks and tails.

23

And oftentimes, in the midst of this cat's mewing, all the rest would suddenly each one in his tune bray forth and incontinently hush again, as it were laughing at somewhat which they heard the other cat declare. And after this sort I beheld them from ten till it was twelve o'clock, at which time, whether it were some vessel in the kitchen under or some board in the printing house hard by I cannot tell, but somewhat fell with such a noise that all the cats got them up upon the house; and I, fearing lest any arose to see what was fallen they would charge me with the hurling down of it if they found me there, I whipped into my chamber quickly and, finding my lamp still burning, I set me down upon my bed and devised upon the doings of these cats, casting all manner of ways what might be conjectured thereof to know what they meant.

[5]
Note here the
painfulness of
the author.

[10]

The good house-
wife's candle
never goeth out.
[15]

And by and by I deemed that the grey cat which sat in the midst was the chief and sat as judge among the rest, and that the cat which continually mewed declared some matter or made account to her of somewhat. By means whereof I was straight caught with such a desire to know what she had said that I could not sleep of all that night, but lay devising by what means I might learn to understand them. And calling to mind that I had read in Albertus Magnus' works a way how to be able to understand birds' voices, I made no more to do, but sought in my library for the little book entitled *De Virtutibus Animalium, etc.*, and greedily read it over. And when I came to "Si vis voces avium intelligere, etc.," Lord how glad I was. And when I had thoroughly marked the description of the medicine, and considered with myself the nature and power of everything therein and how and upon what it wrought, I devised thereby how, with part of those things and additions of other of like virtue and operation, to make a philter for to serve my purpose.

[20]
Earnest desire
banisheth sleep.

Albertus Magnus
teacheth many
wonders.

A philosopher
searcheth the
nature of all
things.

[35]
A description of
the resurrection
of the sun.

And as soon as restless Phoebus was come up out of the smoking sea and, with shaking his golden-

colored beams which were all the night long in Thetis'
moist bosom, had dropped off his silver sweat into
Hera's dry lap, and kissing fair Aurora with glowing
mouth had driven from her the advouterer Lucifer, and
was mounted so high to look upon Europa that, for
all the height of Mile-End steeple, he spied me
through the glass window lying upon my bed, up I
arose and got me abroad to seek for such things as
might serve for the earnest business which I went
about.

    And because you be all my friends that are here I
will hide nothing from you, but declare from point
to point how I behaved myself both in making and
taking my philter. "If thou wilt understand," saith
Albert, "the voices of birds or of beasts, take two in
thy company, and upon Simon and Jude's day early
in the morning, get thee with hounds into a certain
wood, and the first beast that thou meetest take, and
prepare with the heart of a fox, and thou shalt have
thy purpose; and whosoever thou kissest shall understand them as well as thyself."

    Because his writing here is doubtful, because he
saith "quoddam nemus," a certain wood, and because
I knew three men not many years past which, while
they went about this hunting were so 'fraid, whether
with an evil spirit or with their own imagination I
cannot tell, but home they came with their hair
standing on end, and some of them have been the
worse ever since, and their hounds likewise; and seeing
it was so long to St. Jude's Day, therefore I determined
not to hunt at all. But conjecturing that the beast
which they should take was an hedgehog (which at that
time of the year goeth most abroad), and knowing by
reason that the flesh thereof was by nature full of natural heat—and therefore, the principal parts being
eaten, must needs expulse gross matters and subtile
the brain (as by the like power it engendreth fine blood
and helpeth much both against the gout and the

[5]

[10]
*Nothing may be
hid from friends.*

*How to under-
stand birds.*

[20]

*Men and dogs
'fraid out of their
wits in proving
an experiment.*

[30]

*An hedgehog is
one of the plan-
etical beasts, and
therefore good in
magic.*

cramp)—I got me forth towards St. John's Wood, whereas not two days before I had seen one. And see the lucky and unlucky chance! By the way as I went I met with hunters who had that morning killed a fox and three hares, who (I thank them) gave me an hare and the fox's whole body (except the case) and six smart lashes with a slip, because (wherein I did mean no harm) I asked them if they had seen anywhere an hedgehog that morning.

And here, save that my tale is otherwise long, I would show you my mind of these wicked, superstitious observations of foolish hunters, for they be like (as me seemeth) to the papists, which for speaking of good and true words punish good and honest men. Are not apes, owls, cuckoos, bears, and urchins God's good creatures? Why, then, is it not lawful to name them? If they say it bringeth ill luck in the game, then are they unlucky, idolatrical, miscreant infidels and have no true belief in God's providence. I beshrew their superstitious hearts, for my buttocks did bear the burden of their misbelief.

And yet I thank them again for the fox and the hare which they gave me; for with the two hounds at my girdle I went a-hunting, till indeed under an hedge in a hole of the earth by the root of an hollow tree I found an hedgehog with a bushel of crabs about him, whom I killed straight with my knife, saying "Shavol swashmeth, gorgona Iiscud," and with the other beasts, hung him at my girdle, and came homeward as fast as I could hie. But when I came in the close besides Islington, commonly called St. John's Field, a kite, belike very hungry, spied at my back the skinless fox, and thinking to have a morsel strake at it, and that so eagerly that one of his claws was entered so deep that, before he could loose it, I drew out my knife and killed him, saying "Javol sheleg hutotheca Iiscud," and to make up the mess brought him home with the rest.

And ere I had laid them out of my hand, came

Thomas (whom you heard of before) and brought me a cat, which for doing evil turns they had that morning caught in a snare set for her two days before, which for the skin's sake being flain, was so exceeding fat that, after I had taken some of the grease, the inwards, and the head, to make (as I made him believe) a medicine for the gout, they parboiled the rest, and at night, roasted and farced with good herbs, did eat it up every morsel, and was as good meat as was or could be eaten.

One good hap followeth another.

Cat's grease is good for the gout.

A cat was roasted and eaten.
[10]

But now mark! For when Thomas was departed with his cat, I shut my chamber door to me and flayed mine urchin, wishing oft for Doctor Nicholas, or some other expert physician, to make the dissection for the better knowledge of the anatomy. The flesh I washed clean and put it in a pot, and with white wine, Mellisophillos or Melissa (commonly called balm), rosemary, neat's tongue, four parts of the first and two of the second, I made a broth and set it on a fire and boiled it, setting on a limbec, with a glass at the end over the mouth of the pot to receive the water that distilled from it, in the seething whereof I had a pint of a pottle of wine which I put in the pot. Then, because it was about the *solstitium estivale*, and that in confections the hours of the planets must for the better operation be observed, I tarried till ten o'clock before dinner, what time Mercury began his lucky reign.

A solitary man is either a god or a beast.
[15]

Par prior numerus, impar posterior est. gib.

Omne opus fiat in sua planeta. Zoroast.

And then I took a piece of the cat's liver and a piece of the kidney, a piece of the milt and the whole heart, the fox's heart and the lights, the hare's brain, the kite's maw, and the urchin's kidneys. All these I beat in a mortar together until it were small, and then made a cake of it, and baked it upon a hot stone till it was dry like bread. And while this was a-baking I took seven parts of the cat's grease, as much of her brain, with five hairs of her beard (three black and two grey), three parts of the fox's grease, as much of the brain, with the hoofs of his left feet, the like portion of the

Omne totum totaliter malum. Trismeg.
[30]

Deus impari numero gaudet.

urchin's grease and brain with his stones, all the kite's brain, with all the marrow of her bones, the juice of her heart, her upper beak and the middle claw of her left foot, the fat of the hare's kidneys and the juice of his right shoulder bone. All these things I pounded together in a mortar by the space of an hour, and then I put it in a cloth and hung it over a basin in the sun, out of which dropped within four hours after about half a pint of oil very fair and clear.

Then took I the galls of all these beasts, and the kite's toe, and served them likewise, keeping the liquor that dropped from them. At twelve of the clock, what time the sun began his planetical dominion, I went to dinner. But meat I ate none, save the boiled urchin; my bread was the cake mentioned before; my drink was the distillation of the urchin's broth, which was exceeding strong and pleasant both in taste and savor.

After that I had dined well, my head waxed so heavy that I could not choose but sleep. And after that I waked again, which was within an hour. My mouth and my nose purged exceedingly such yellow, white, and tawny matters as I never saw before, nor thought that any such had been in man's body. When a pint of this gear was come forth my rheum ceased, and my head and all my body was in exceeding good temper, and a thousand things which I had not thought of in twenty years before came so freshly to my mind as if they had been then presently done, heard, or seen. Whereby I perceived that my brain (chiefly the nuke memorative) was marvelously well purged. My imagination also was so fresh that by and by I could show a probable reason what, and in what sort, and upon what matter, everything which I had taken wrought, and the cause why.

Then, to be occupied after my sleep, I cast away the carcass of the fox and of the kite, with all the garbage both of them and of the rest, saving the tongues and the ears which were very necessary for my purpose. And

Dextra bona bonis sinistra vero sinistris.
[5]

Calor solis est ignis alichimistice distillationis.
[10]

Master Streamer varieth from the astronomers in his planet hours.

The intelligible diet.
[20]

There be many strange humors in many men's heads.

The remembrance lieth in the noodle of the head.

A good philosopher.

Exercise is good after sleep.

thus I prepared them: I took all the ears and scalded off the hair; then stamped I them in a mortar; and when they were all a dry jelly, I put to them rue, fennel, lowache, and leek blades, of each an handful, and pounded them afresh. Then divided I all the matter into two equal parts, and made two little pillows and stuffed them therewith. And when Saturn's dry hour of dominion approached, I fried these pillows in good oil olive and laid them hot to mine ears, to each ear one, and kept them thereto till nine o'clock at night, which holp exceedingly to comfort my understanding power. But, because as I perceived the cell perceptible of my brain intelligible was yet too gross, by means that the filmy pannicle coming from *dura mater* made too strait oppilations by ingrossing the pores and conduits imaginative, I devised to help that with this gargaristical fume, whose subtle ascension is wonderful. I took the cat's, the fox's, and the kite's tongue and sod them in wine well near to jelly. Then I took them out of the wine and put them in a mortar and added to them of new cat's dung an ounce; of mustard seed, garlic, and pepper as much; and when they were with beating incorped, I made lozenges and trochisks thereof.

And at six o'clock at night, what time the sun's dominion began again, I supped with the rest of the meat which I left at dinner. And when Mercury's reign approached, which was within two hours after, I drank a great draught of my stilled water, and anointed all my head over with the wine and oil before described, and with the water which came out of the galls I washed mine eyes. And because no humors should ascend into my head by evaporation of my reins through the chine bone, I took an ounce of Alkakengi in powder, which I had for a like purpose not two days afore bought at the 'pothecaries, and therewith rubbed and chafed my back from the neck down to the middle, and heated in a frying pan my pillows afresh,

Hot things purge the head.

[5]

A good medicine for aching ears.

What hindreth the imaginative power.

[20]
The wholesome things are not always most toothsome.
[25]

Mercury furthereth all fine and subtle practices.
[30]

The chiefest point of wisdom is to prevent inconveniences.

Heat augmenteth the virtue of out- ward plasters.

The ungracious should be ungra- ciously served.

[10]
Strange things are delectable.

We laugh gladly at shrewd turns.

[20]

[25]

[30]
Good success of things maketh men joyous. Saturn is a cold, old planet.

and laid them to mine ears, and tied a kercher about my head, and with my lozenges and trochisks in a box, I went out among the servants, among whom was a shrewd boy, a very crack-rope, that needs would know what was in my box. And I, to sauce him after his sau- ciness, called them ''presciencial pills,'' affirming that whoso might eat one of them should not only under- stand wonders, but also prophesy after them. Where- upon the boy was exceeding earnest in entreating me to give him one; and when at last very loathly, as it seemed, I granted his request, he took a lozenge, and put it in his mouth, and chewed it apace, by means whereof when the fume ascended he began to spattle and spit, saying, ''By God's bones, it is a cat's turd.'' At this the company laughed apace; and so did I too, verifying it to be as he said, and that he was a prophet.

But that he might not spew too much by imagina- tion, I took a lozenge in my mouth and kept it under my tongue, showing thereby that it was not evil. While this pastime endured, methought I heard one cry with a loud voice, ''What Isegrim, what Isegrim''; and therefore I asked whose name was Isegrim, saying that one did call him. But they said that they knew none of that name, nor heard any that did call. ''No,'' quod I (for it called still), ''Hear you nobody? Who is that called so loud?''

''We hear nothing but a cat,'' quod they, ''which meweth above in the leads.''

When I saw it was so indeed, and that I understood what the cat said, glad was I as any man alive. And taking my leave of them as though I would to bed straight, I went into my chamber (for it was past nine of the clock). And because the hour of Saturnus' cold dominion approached, I put on my gown and got me privily to the place in the which I had viewed the cats the night before. And when I had settled myself where I might conveniently hear and see all things done in

the leads where this cat cried still for Isegrim, I put
into my two nostrils two trochisks and into my mouth
two lozenges, one above my tongue the other under;
and put off my left shoe, because of Jupiter's
appropinquation; and laid the fox tail under my foot.
And to hear the better, I took off my pillows which
stopped mine ears; and then listened and viewed as
attentively as I could.

*There is great
cunning in due
applying of
medicines.*

But I warrant you the pellicle, or filmy rime, that
lyeth within the bottom of mine ear hole, from whence
little veins carry the sounds to the senses, was with this
medicine in my pillows so purged and parched, or at
least dried, that the least moving of the air, whether
struck with breath of living creatures, which we call
voices, or with the moving of dead (as winds, waters,
trees, carts, falling of stones, etc.), which are named
noises, sounded so shrill in my head by reverberation
of my 'fined films, that the sound of them altogether
was so disordered and monstrous that I could discern
no one from other, save only the harmony of the
moving of the spheres, which noise excelled all other
as much both in pleasance and shrill highness of sound
as the Zodiac itself surmounteth all other creatures in
altitude of place. For in comparison of the basest of
this noise, which is the moving of Saturn by means
of his large compass, the highest voices of birds and
the straitest whistling of the wind, or any other organ
pipes whose sounds I heard confused together,
appeared but a low bass. And yet was those an high
treble to the voice of beasts, to which as a mean the
running of rivers was a tenor; and the boiling of the
sea and the cataracts or gulfs thereof a goodly bass;
and the rushing, brising, and falling of the clouds a
deep diapason.

*The cause of
hearing.*

*The difference
between voices
and noises.*

*The harmony of
heaven excelleth
all other.*

[25]

*The harmony
of elemental
mixtures.*
[30]

While I harkened to this broil, laboring to discern
both voices and noises asunder, I heard such a mixture
as I think was never in Chaucer's House of Fame; for
there was nothing within an hundred mile of me done

[35]

*Chaucer's House
of Fame.*

At every hundred mile the air reflecteth by means of the roundness of the world.

The cart and cucking stool groveth for such.

Here the poetical fury came upon him.

Many noises in the night which all men hear not.

Over much noise maketh one deaf.

Heat shrilleth all moist instruments.

[35]

All sudden things astonish us.

on any side (for from so far, but no farther, the air may come because of obliquation) but I heard it as well as if I had been by it, and could discern all voices, but by means of noises understand none. Lord what ado women made in their beds—some scolding; some laughing; some weeping; some singing to their sucking children, which made a woeful noise with their continual crying. And one shrewd wife a great way off (I think at St. Albans) called her husband "cuckold" so loud and shrilly that I heard that plain; and would fain have heard the rest, but could not by no means for barking of dogs, grunting of hogs, wawling of cats, rumbling of rats, gaggling of geese, humming of bees, rousing of bucks, gaggling of ducks, singing of swans, ringing of pans, crowing of cocks, sewing of socks, cackling of hens, scrabbling of pens, peeping of mice, trulling of dice, curling of frogs, and toads in the bogs, chirking of crickets, shutting of wickets, shriking of owls, flittering of fowls, routing of knaves, snorting of slaves, farting of churls, fizzling of girls, with many things else—as ringing of bells, counting of coins, mounting of groins, whispering of lovers, springling of plovers, groaning and spewing, baking and brewing, scratching and rubbing, watching and shrugging— with such a sort of commixed noises as would a-deaf anybody to have heard; much more me, seeing that the pannicles of mine ears were with my medicine made so fine and stiff, and that by the temperate heat of the things therein, that like a tabor dried before the fire or else a lute string by heat shrunk nearer, they were incomparably amended in receiving and yielding the shrillness of any touching sounds.

While I was earnestly harkening, as I said, to hear the woman, minding nothing else, the greatest bell in St. Botolph's steeple, which is hard by, was tolled for some rich body that then lay in passing, the sound whereof came with such a rumble into mine ear that I thought all the devils in Hell had broken loose and were come about me, and was so afraid therewith that, when I felt the foxtail under my foot (which through fear I had forgot), I deemed it had been the Devil indeed. And therefore I cried out as loud as ever I could, "The Devil, the Devil, the Devil!" But when some of the folks, raised with my noise, had sought me in my chamber and found me not there, they went seeking about, calling one to another, "Where is he? Where is he? I cannot find Master Streamer." Which noise and stir of them was so great in mine ears and passing man's common sound, that I thought they had been devils indeed which sought and asked for me.

[5]

[10]
Fertilitas sibi ipsi nocus.

Wherefore I crept close into a corner in the chimney and hid me, saying many good prayers to save me from them. And because their noise was so terrible that I could not abide it, I thought best to stop mine ears, thinking thereby I should be the less afraid. And as I was thereabout, a crow, which belike was nodding asleep on the chimney top, fell down into the chimney over my head, whose flittering in the fall made such a noise that, when I felt his feet upon my head, I thought that the Devil had been come indeed and seized upon me. And when I cast up my hand to save me, and therewith touched him, he called me "knave" in his language, after such a sort that I swooned for fear. And by that I was come to myself again, he was flowen from me into the chamber roof, and there he sat all night.

Danger maketh men devout.

How evil haps run together.

A man may die only by imagination of harm.

Then took I my pillows to stop mine ears; for the rumble that the servants made I took for the devils, it was so great and shrill. And I had no sooner put them on, but by and by I heard it was the servants which sought for me, and that I was deceived through my clearness of hearing, for the bell which put me in all this fear (for which I never loved bells since) tolled still, and I perceived well enough what it was. And seeing that the servants would not leave calling and seeking till they found me, I went down to them

[30]

We hate forever whatsoever hath harmed us.

and feigned that a cat had been in my chamber and
'fraid me. Whereupon they went to bed again, and
I to mine old place.

THE THIRD PART OF
MASTER STREAMER'S ORATION

By this time waning Cynthia, which the day before had filled her growing horns, was come upon our hemisphere and freshly yielded forth her brother's light, which the reverberation of Thetis' trembling face, now full by means of spring, had fully cast upon her, whereof she must needs lose every day more and more, by means the neap abasing Thetis' swollen face would make her to cast beyond her those rades, which before the full the spring had caused her to throw short—like as, with a crystal glass a man may, by the placing of it either high or low, so cast the sun or a candlelight upon any round glass of water that it shall make the light thereof both in waxing and waning to counterfeit the moon. For you shall understand—chiefly you, Master Willot, that are my lord's astronomer—that all our ancestors have failed in knowledge of natural causes; for it is not the moon that causeth the sea to ebb and flow, neither to neap and spring, but the neaping and springing of the sea is the cause of the moon's both waxing and waning. For the moonlight is nothing save the shining of the sun cast into the element by opposition of the sea; as also the stars are nothing else but the sunlight reflected upon the face of rivers and cast upon the crystalline heaven, which because rivers alway keep like course, therefore are the stars alway of one bigness. As for the course of the stars, from east to west is natural by means of the sun's like moving; but in that they ascend and descend (that is, sometime come northward and sometime go southward), that is caused also by the sun's being either on this side or on the other side his line like-nightical. The like reason followeth for the

The description of the moon at full.

[10]
How to counterfeit the moon.

Astronomers are deceived.

The spring and neaping of the sea causeth the moon to wax and wane.

What the moon and stars be.
[25]

The sun's moving is cause of divers moving of the stars.

35

Why the poles do not move.

poles not moving, and that is the situation of those rivers or dead seas which cast them and the roundness and egg-form of the firmament. But to let this pass, which in my *Book of Heaven and Hell* shall be plainly not only declared but both by reason and experience proved, I will come again to my matter.

I take this book to be it that is entitled Of the Great Egg.

When Cynthia, I say, as following her brother's steps, had looked in at my chamber window and saw me neither in my bed nor at my book, she hied her apace into the south, and at a little hole in the house roof peeped in and saw me where I was set to harken to the cats. And by this time all the cats which were there the night before were assembled with many other, only the great grey one excepted. Unto whom, as soon as he was come, all the rest did their 'beisance as they did the night before. And when he was set, thus he began in his language (which I understood as well as if he had spoken English).

The man is studious.

Light searcheth all things.

[15]
Good manners among cats.

"Ah my dear friends and fellows, you may say I have been a lingerer this night and that I have tarried long; but you must pardon me for I could come no sooner. For when this evening I went into an ambry where was much good meat to steal my supper, there came a wench not thinking I had been there and clapped the lid down, by means whereof I have had much to do to get forth. Also, in the way as I came hither over the housetops, in a gutter were thieves breaking in at the window, who 'fraid me so that I lost my way and fell down into the street and had much to do to escape the dogs. But seeing that by the grace of Hagat and Heg I am now come, although I perceive by the tail of the Great Bear and by Alhabor, which are now somewhat southward, that the fifth hour of our night approacheth; yet, seeing this is the last night of my charge and that tomorrow I must again to my lord Cammoloch (at this all the cats spread along their tails and cried, 'Hagat and Heg save him'), go to now good Mouse-slayer," quod he, "and that time which my

The strange hap of Grisard.

Sweet meat must have sour sauce.
[25]
Cats are afraid of thieves.
Hagat and Heg are witches which the cats do worship.

Cats are skilled in astronomy.
[35]
Cammoloch is chief prince among cats.

misfortune hath lost, recover again by the briefness of thy talk.''

"I will my lord," quod Mouse-slayer, which is the cat which as I told you stood before the great cat the night before continually mewing; who in her language, after that with her tail she had made courtesy, shrunk in her neck and said, "Whereas by virtue of your commission from my lord Cammoloch (whose life Hagat and Heg defend), who by inheritance and our free election enjoyeth the empire of his traitorously murdered mother the goddess Grimolochin, you his greffier and chief counselor, my lord Grisard, with Isegrim and Pol-noir your assistants, upon a complaint put up in your high dais by that false accuser Catch-rat, who beareth me malice because I refused his lecherously offered delights, have caused me, in purging of myself before this honorable company, to declare my whole life since the blind days of my kitlinghood. You remember, I trust, how in the two nights passed I have declared my life for four years' space, wherein you perceive how I behaved me all that time.

"Wherefore, to begin where I left last, ye shall understand that my lord and lady, whose lives I declared unto you last yesternight, left the city and went to dwell in the country, and carried me with them. And being there strange I lost their house, and with Bird-hunt my mate, the gentlest in honest venery that ever I met with, went to a town where he dwelt called Stratford—either Stony, upon Tine, or upon Avon, I do not well remember which—where I dwelled half a year— and this was in the time when preachers had leave to speak against the Mass, but it was not forbidden till half a year after. In this time I saw nothing worthy to certify my lord of, save this.

"My dame, with whom I dwelt, and her husband were both old, and therefore hard to be turned from their rooted belief which they had in the Mass, which caused divers young folk, chiefly their sons and a

Gentleness becometh officers.

[5]

Mouse-slayer telleth on her story.
[10]
Grimolochin is the same that was late called Grimalkin.
[15]
She purgeth herself by declaring her life.

[20]

Mouse-slayer was by her mistress carried into the country.

Bird-hunt was Mouse-slayer's mate.
[30]

[35]
Old errors are hard to be removed.

learned kinsman of theirs, to be the more earnest to teach and persuade them. And when they had almost brought the matter to a good point, I cannot tell how it chanced, but my dame's sight failed her, and she was so sick that she kept her bed two days. Wherefore she sent for the parish priest, her old ghostly father; and when all were voided the chamber save I and they two, she told him how sick she was and how blind, so that she could see nothing, and desired him to pray for her and give her good counsel. To whom he said thus, 'It is no marvel though you be sick and blind in body which suffer your soul willingly to be blinded. You send for me now, but why send you not for me when these new heretics teach you to leave the Catholic belief of Christ's flesh in the sacrament?' 'Why sir,' quod she, 'I did send for you once, and when you came they posed you so with Holy Writ and saints' writings that you could say nothing but call them "heretics," and that they had made the New Testament themselves.'

'' 'Yea,' quod he, 'but did I not bid you take heed then, and told you how God would plague you?' 'Yes, good sir,' quod she, 'you did, and now to my pain I find you too true a prophet. But I beseech you forgive me and pray to God for me, and whatsoever you will teach me, that will I believe unto the death.' 'Well,' quod he, 'God refuseth no sinners that will repent, and therefore in any case believe that Christ's flesh, body, soul, and bone is as it was born of our Blessed Lady in the consecrated Host, and see that therefore you worship it, pray, and offer to it. For by it any of your friends' souls may be brought out of Purgatory (which these new heretics say is no place at all—but when their souls fry in it, they shall tell me another tale). And that you may know that all I say is true, and that the Mass can deliver such as trust in it from all manner of sins, I will by and by say you a Mass that shall restore your sight and health.'

A sudden disease.

[5]

Cats are admitted to all secrets.

A jolly, persuading knave.

[15]

Railing and slandering are the Papists' Scriptures.

A true coal prophet.

Ghostly counsel of a Popish confessor.

No such persuasion as miracles chiefly in helping one from grief.

"Then took he out of his bosom a wafer cake and called for wine. And then, shutting the door unto him, revised himself in a surplice, and upon a table set before the bed he laid his porteous, and thereout he said Mass. And when he came to the elevation, he lifted up the cake and said to my dame (which in two days afore saw nothing), 'Wipe thine eyes thou sinful woman and look upon thy Maker.' With that she lifted up herself and saw the cake, and had her sight and her health as well as ever she had before. When Mass was done she thanked God and him exceedingly, and he gave charge that she should tell to no young folks how she was holp, for his bishop had throughout the diocese forbidden them to say or sing any Mass, but commanded her that secretly unto old honest men and women she should at all times most devoutly rehearse it. And by reason of this miracle, many are so confirmed in that belief that, although by a common law all Masses upon penalty were since forbidden, divers have them privily and nightly said in their chambers until this day.

" 'Marry sir,' quod Pol-noir, 'this was either a mighty miracle or else a mischievous subtlety of a magistical minister. But sure if the priest by magical art blinded her not afore, and so by like magical sorcery cured her again, it were as good for us to hire him or other priests at our delivery to sing a Mass before our kitlings, that they might in their birth be delivered of their blindness. And sure, if I knew the priest, it should scape me hard but I would have one litter of kitlings in some chamber where he useth now to say his privy night Masses.' 'What need that?' quod Mouse-slayer, 'it would do them no good. For I myself, upon like consideration, kittened since in another mistress's chamber of mine where a priest every day said Mass; but my kitlings saw naught the better, but rather the worse.'

"But when I heard that the Lord with whom I went

Veritas quaerit angulos.

[5]

A young knave made an old woman's maker.
[10]

Old folk are lighter of credit than young.

Cats hear many privy night Masses.

Sorcerers may make folk blind.

Why Masses may serve well.

[30]

Devout kitlings that heard Mass so young.

Flatterers are dili-
gent when they
spy a profit.

[5]

into the country would to London to dwell again, I
kept the house so well for a month before that my Lady
when she went carried me with her. And when I was
come to London again, I went in visitation to mine
old acquaintance. And when I was great with kitling,
because I would not be unpurveyed of a place to kitten
in, I got in favor and household with an old gentlewoman, a widow, with whom I passed out this whole
year.

The trade of an
old gentlewoman.

"This woman got her living by boarding young gentlemen, for whom she kept always fair wenches in store,
for whose sake she had the more resort. And to tell
you the truth of her trade, it was fine and crafty, and
not so dangerous as deceitful. For when she had soaked

Whores, gaming,
and good hos-
tesses make many
gentlemen make
shameful shifts.
[20]

from young gentlemen all that they had, then would
she cast them off, except they fell to cheating. Wherefore many of them in the nighttime would go abroad
and bring the next morning home with them sometimes money, sometime jewels (as rings or chains),
sometime apparel; and sometime they would come
again cursing their ill fortune, with nothing save per-

All is fish that
cometh to
the net.
[25]

adventure dry blows or wet wounds. But whatsoever
they brought, my dame would take it and find the
means either so to gage it that she would never fetch
it again, or else melt it and sell it to the goldsmiths.

A Catholic queen.

"And notwithstanding that she used these wicked
practices, yet was she very holy and religious. And
therefore, although that all images were forbidden, yet
kept she one of Our Lady in her coffer. And every

[30]

night, when everybody were gone to bed and none in
her chamber but she and I, then would she fetch Her

Images cannot
see to hear,
except they have
much light.

out, and set Her upon her cupboard, and light up two
or three wax candles afore Her, and then kneel down
to Her, sometime an whole hour, saying over her beads
and praying Her to be good unto her and to save her
and all her guests both from danger and shame, and

Our Lady is hired
to play the bawd.

promising that then she would honor and serve Her
during all her life.

"While I was with this woman I was alway much cherished and made of, for on nights while she was a-praying, I would be playing with her beads and alway catch them as she let them fall, and would sometime put my head in the compass of them and run away with them about my neck, whereat many times she took great pleasure, yea and so did Our Lady too. For my dame would say sometimes to Her, 'Yea, Blessed Lady, I know thou hearest me by thy smiling at my cat.'

"And never did my dame do me any hurt save once, and that I was even with her for; and that was thus. There was a gentleman, one of her boarders, much enamored in the beauty of a merchantman's wife in the city, whom he could by no means persuade to satisfy his lust. Yea, when he made her great banquets, offered her rich apparel and all kind of jewels precious which commonly women delight in, yea and large sums of money which corrupt even the gods themselves, yet could he by no means alter her mind, so much she esteemed her good name and honesty. Wherefore, forced through desire of that which he could not but long for, and so much the more because it was most earnestly denied him, he brake his mind to my dame, and entreated her to aid him to win this young woman's favor, and promised her for her labor whatsoever she would require.

"Whereupon my dame, which was taken for as honest as any in the city, found the means to desire this young woman to a dinner. And against she should come, my dame gave me a piece of pudding which she had filled full of mustard, which as soon as I had eaten wrought so in my head that it made mine eyes run all the day after; and to mend this she blew pepper in my nose to make me neese. And when the young wife was come, after that my dame had showed her all the commodities of her house (for women delight much to show forth what they have), they set them down together at the table, none save only they two.

Old women love their cats well.

[5]
The image laughed to see the cat play with her dame's beads.
[10]

Love is loiterers' occupation.

An honest wife.

Quid non mortalia pectora cogis, auri sacra fames?
[20]

[25]

All is not gold that glistereth.

[30]
Mustard purgeth the head and pepper maketh one neese.
[35]
Women are glorious.

Gossips'
common chat.

[5]
Women can weep
when they will.

There is no deceit
to the cheat of
an old bawd.

A shameful lie
shamefully
set forth.

Tears move young
minds lightly.

Women are
orators by nature.

[30]

All women ought
above all things
to esteem their
honesty.

And while they were in gossips' talk about the behaviors of this woman and that, I came as I was accustomed and sat by my dame. And when the young woman, hearing me cough and seeing me weep continually, asked what I ailed, my dame, who had tears at her commandment, sighed and, fallen as it were into a sudden dump, brast forth a-weeping and said: 'In faith, mistress, I think I am the infortunatest woman alive, upon whom God hath at once poured forth all his plagues. For my husband, the honestest man that lived, He hath taken from me; and with him mine heir and only son, the most towardly young man that was alive; and yet, not satisfied herewith, lo here my only daughter, which (though I say it) was as fair a woman and as fortunately married as any in this city, He hath, for her honesty or cruelty I cannot tell whether, turned into this likeness, wherein she hath been above this two months, continually weeping as you see and lamenting her miserable wretchedness.'

"The young woman, astonished at this tale, and crediting it by means of my dame's lachrymable protestion and deep dissimulation, asked her the more earnestly how and by what chance, and for what cause as she thought, she was so altered. 'Ah,' quod my dame, 'as I said before, I cannot tell what I should think; whether excuse my daughter and accuse God, or else blame her and acquit Him. For this my daughter, being as I said fortunately married, and so beloved of her husband and loving again to him as now we both too late do and forever I think shall rue, was loved exceedingly of another young man, who made great suit and labor unto her. But she, as I think all women should, esteeming her honesty and promise made to her husband the day of their marriage, refused still his desire. But because he was importunate, she came at last and told me it. And I, thinking that I did well, charged her in any case (which full oft since I have repented) that she should not consent unto him,

but to shake him off with shrewd words and
threatening answers. She did so; alas, alas the while.
And the young man, seeing none other boot, went
home and fell sick; and loving so honestly and secretly
that he would make none other of his counsel, forpined and languished upon his bed the space of three
days, receiving neither meat nor drink. And then, per-
ceiving his death to approach, he wrote a letter, which
I have in my purse, and sent it by his boy to my
daughter. If you can read you shall see it; I cannot,
but my daughter here could very well, and write too.'
Herewith my dame wept apace, and took the letter
out of her purse and gave it this young woman, who
read it in form following.

> The Nameless Lover to the Nameless
> Beloved, in whose love, sith he may not live,
> he only desireth license to die.

> Cursed be the woeful time wherein mutual
> love first mixed the mass of my miserable
> carcass. Cursed be the hour that ever the fatal
> destinies have ought for me purveyed. Yea,
> cursed be the unhappy hour, may I say,
> in which I first saw those piercing eyes
> which, by insensible and unquenchable
> power inflaming my heart to desire, are so
> blind of all mercy as will rather with rigor
> consume my life than rue my grief with one
> drop of pity. I sue not to you, my dear
> unloving love, for any kind of grace, the
> doubtful hope whereof despair hath long
> since with the pouring showers of cruel
> words utterly quenched. But thus much I
> desire, which also by right me thinketh my
> faithful love hath well deserved, that sith
> your fidelity in wedlock (which I can and
> must needs praise, as would to God I could
> not) will suffer my pined corse no longer
> to retain the breath through cold cares

*Sharp words
and threatening
answers will soon
cool adulterers.*

[10]
*It is as much pity
to see a woman
weep as to see a
goose go barefoot.*
[15]

[20]

[25]

[30]

[35]

wholly consumed, yet at the least, which is
also an office of friendship before the gods
meritorious, come visit him, who if ought
might quench love should not love, whose

[5]   mouth these three days hath taken no food,
whose eyes the like time have taken no rest,
whose heart this three weeks was never
merry, whose mind these three months was
never quiet, whose bed this seven nights was

[10]   never made, and who (to be brief) is in all
parts so enfeebled that living he dieth and
dead awhile he liveth. And when this silly
ghost shall leave this cruel and miserable
prison, in recompense of his love, life, and

[15]   death, let those white and tender hands of
yours close up those open windows through
which the uncomfortable light of your
beauty shone first into his heart. If you
refuse this to do, I beseech the gods immor-

[20]   tal, to whom immediately I go, that as
without any kind of either love or kindness
you have caused me to die, so that none
other caught with your beauty do likewise
perish; I beseech (I say) the just gods that

[25]   either they change that honest stony heart,
or else disfigure that fair merciless favor.
Thus, for want of force either to endite or
write any more, I take my leave, desiring
you either to come and see me die, or if I

[30]   be dead before, to see me honestly buried.
Yours unregarded alive.   G.S.

A tender heart is   "When the young woman had read this letter, she
easily pierced.   took it again to my dame, and with much to do to
withhold her swelling tears, she said, 'I am sorry for

[35]   your heaviness, much more for this poor man's, but
most of all for your daughter's. But what did she after
she saw this letter?' 'Ah,' quod my dame, 'she
esteemed it as she did his suits before. She sent him

a rough answer in writing; but or ever the boy came home with it, his master was dead. Within two days after, my son-in-law (her husband) died suddenly. And within two days after, as she sat here with me lamenting his death, a voice cried aloud, "Ah, flinty heart, repent thy cruelty." And immediately (oh extreme rigor) she was changed as you now see her. Whereupon I gather that though God would have us keep our faith to our husbands, yet rather than any other should die for our sakes, we should not make any conscience to save their lives. For it fareth in this point as it doth in all other; for as all extremities are vices, so is it a vice, as appeareth plainly by the punishment of my daughter, to be too extreme in honesty, chastity, or any other kind of virtue.'

"This, with other talk of my dame in the dinner time, so sank into the young woman's mind that the same afternoon she sent for the gentleman whom she had erst so constantly refused and promised him that, if he would appoint her an unsuspected place, she would be glad to meet him to fulfill all his lust, which he appointed to be the next day at my dame's house. Where, when they were all assembled, I, minding to acquit my dame for giving me mustard, caught a quick mouse, whereof my dame always was exceedingly afraid, and came with it under her clothes and there let it go, which immediately crope up upon her leg. But Lord, how she bestirred her then; how she cried out; and how pale she looked. And I, to amend the matter, making as though I leaped at the mouse, all to-bescrat her thighs and her belly, so that I dare say she was not whole again in two months after. And when the young woman, to whom she showed her pounced thighs, said I was an unnatural daughter to deal so with my mother, 'Nay, nay,' quod she, 'I cannot blame her, for it was through my counsel that she suffered all this sorrow. And yet I dare say she did it against her will, thinking to have caught the mouse,

Women's answers are never to seek.

[5]

Note the craft of a bawd.

All extremities are to be forsaken.
[15]
Evil communication confoundeth good virtues.

[20]

Cats are malicious.

Women are afraid of their own shadows.
[30]
The cat payeth her dame for her mustard.
It is an unnatural child that will hurt the mother.

Let young women take heed of old bawds.

[5]

Cats have laws among them which they keep better than we do ours.

He that despiseth those that love him shall be despised of them that he loveth.

Cats do long while they be with kitten.

There be churls among cats as well as among Christian folk.

It is the conceit of a thing and not the thing itself that is longed for.

Churls must be churlishly served.

which else I dare say would have crept into my belly.' By this means was this innocent woman, otherwise invincible, brought to consent to commit whoredom.

"Shortly after, this young woman begged me of my dame; and to her I went, and dwelled with her all that year. In which year, as all the cats in the parish can tell, I never disobeyed or transgressed our holy law in refusing the concupiscential company of any cat nor the act of generation, although sometimes it were more painful to me than pleasant, if it were offered in due and convenient time. Indeed, I confess I refused Catch-rat, and bit him and scrat him, which our law forbiddeth. For on a time this year when I was great with kitlings, which he of a proud stomach refused to help to get, although I earnestly wooed him thereto; what time he loved so much his own daughter Slick-skin that all other seemed vile in his sight, which also esteemed him as much as he did the rest—that is, never a whit. In this time (I say) when I was great with kitling, I found him in a gutter eating a bat which he had caught that evening; and as you know not only we, but also women in our case, do oft long for many things, so I then longed for a piece of the reremouse, and desired him, for saving of my kitten, to give me a morsel, though it were but of the leather-like wing. But he, like an unnatural, ravenous churl, eat it all up and would give me none. And as men do nowadays to their wives, he gave me bitter words, saying we longed for wantonness and not for any need. This grieved me so sore, chiefly for the lack of that I longed for, that I was sick two days after, and had not it been for good dame Isegrim, who brought me a piece of a mouse and made me believe it was of a back, I had lost by burden by kittening ten days before my time.

"When I was recovered and went abroad again, about three days, this cruel churl met me and needs would have been doing with me. To whom, when I had made answer according to his deserts, and told

him withall, which he might see too by my belly what
case I was in, tush, there was no remedy (I think he
had eaten savory), but for all that I could say, he would
have his will. I, seeing that, and that he would ravish
me perforce, I cried out for help as loud as ever I could
squawl, and to defend myself till succor came I scrat
and bit as hard as ever I could. And this notwithstanding, had not Isegrim and her son Lightfoot come
the sooner (who both are here and can witness), he
would have marred me quite. Now, whether I might
in this case refuse him, and do as I did without breach
of our holy law, which forbiddeth us females to refuse
any males not exceeding the number of ten in a night,
judge you, my lords, to whom the interpretation of
the laws belongeth.

" 'Yes, surely,' quod Grisard, 'for in the third year
of the reign of Glascalon, at a court holden in Cat-
wood, as appeareth in the records, they decreed upon
that exception, forbidding any male in this case to force
any female, and that upon great penalties. But to let
this pass, whereof we were satisfied in your purgation
the first night, tell us how you behaved you with your
new mistress, and that as briefly as you can; for lo
where Corleonis is almost plain west, whereby ye know
the goblins' hour approacheth.'

"After I was come to my young mistress," quod
Mouse-slayer, "she made much of me, thinking that
I had been my old dame's daughter, and many tales
she told thereof to her gossips. My master also made
much of me, because I would take meat in my foot
and therewith put it in my mouth and feed. In this
house dwelt an ungracious fellow who, delighting
much in unhappy turns, on a time took four walnut
shells and filled them full of soft pitch, and put them
upon my feet, and then put my feet into cold water
till the pitch was hardened, and then he let me go.
But Lord, how strange it was to me to go in shoes, and
how they vexed me, for when I ran upon any steep

*Savory is an hot
herb provoking
lust in cats.*

[10]

*A law for adul-
tery among cats.*

[15]

*Glascalon was
chief prince of
the cats after
Grimolochin.*

*After one a clock
at midnight the
goblins go abroad,
and as soon as
any cock croweth,
which is their
hour, that is at
three, they return
homeward.*

*Divers men
delight in divers
fond things.*
[35]
A cat was shoed.

thing they made me slide and fall down. Wherefore all that afternoon, for anger that I could not get off my shoes, I hid me in a corner of the garret which was boarded, under which my master and mistress lay. And

at night when they were all in bed, I spied a mouse playing in the floor; and when I ran at her to catch her, my shoes made such a noise upon the boards that it waked my master, who was a man very fearful of spirits. And when he with his servants harkened well

to the noise, which went pit-pat, pit-pat, as it had been the trampling of an horse, they waxed all afraid and said surely it was the Devil.

"And as one of them, an hardy fellow (even he that had shoed me), came upstairs to see what it was, I went

downward to meet him and made such a rattling that, when he saw my glistering eyes, he fell down backward and brake his head, crying out, 'The Devil, the Devil, the Devil.' Which his master and all the rest hearing, ran naked as they were into the street and

cried the same cry.

"Whereupon the neighbors arose and called up, among other, an old priest, who lamented much the

lack of holy water which they were forbidden to make. Howbeit, he went to church and took out of the font some of the christening water, and took his chalice, and therein a wafer unconsecrate, and put on a sur-

plice, and his stole about his neck, and fet out of his chamber a piece of holy candle which he had kept two year. And herewith he came to the house, and with his candle-light in the one hand and a holy-water sprinkle in the other hand, and his chalice and wafer in sight of his bosom, and a pot of font-water at his girdle, up he came praying towards the garret, and all the people after him.

"And when I saw this, and thinking I should have seen some Mass that night, as many nights before in other places I had, I ran towards them thinking to meet them. But when the priest heard me come, and

by a glimpsing had seen me, down he fell upon them
that were behind him, and with his chalice hurt one,
with his water pot another, and his holy candle fell
into another priest's breech beneath (who, while the
rest were hawsoning me, was conjuring our maid at
the stair foot) and all to-besinged him, for he was so
afraid with the noise of the rest which fell that he had
not the power to put it out. When I saw all this business, down I ran among them where they lay on heaps.
But such a fear as they were all in then I think was
never seen afore; for the old priest, which was so tum-
bled among them that his face lay upon a boy's bare
arse, which belike was fallen headlong under him, was
so astonished that, when the boy, which for fear had
beshit himself, had all to-rayed his face, he neither
felt nor smelt it, nor removed from him.

Priests have been good conjurers of such kind of spirits.

[10]

"Then went I to my dame, which lay among the
rest God knoweth very madly, and so mewed and
curled about her that at last she said, 'I ween it be
my cat.' That hearing the knave that had shoed me,
and calling to mind that erst he had forgot, said it
was so indeed and nothing else. That hearing the
priest, in whose holy breech the holy candle all this
while lay burning, he took heart a grace, and before
he was spied rose up and took the candle in his hand,
and looked upon me and all the company, and fell
a-laughing at the handsome lying of his fellow's face.
The rest, hearing him, came every man to himself and
arose and looked upon me, and cursed the knave
which had shoed me, who would in no case be a-
known of it. This done, they got hot water and dissolved the pitch and plucked off my shoes. And then
every man (after they desired each other not to be a-
known of this night's work) for shame departed to their
lodgings, and all our household went to bed again."

Fear taketh away the senses.

[20]
A liar and a doer of shrewd turns ought to have a good memory.
[25]
One hardy man encourageth many cowards.

[30]

When all the cats, and I too for company, had
laughed at this space, Mouse-slayer proceeded and said,
"After this about three-quarters of a year, which was

Silence is the best friend that shame hath. The author laughed in a cat's voice.

Adulterers are diligent in waiting their times.

A wanton wife and a back door will soon make a rich man poor.

Chance oftentimes betrayeth evil.

None seem outwardly so loving as whores.

Sine Baccho et cetera friget Venus.

Fear overcometh smart.

All are not mice that are behind painted cloths.
[35]
It is justice to punsh those parts that offend.

at Whitsuntide last, I played another prank, and that was this. The gentleman, who by mine old dame's lying and my weeping was accepted and retained of my mistress, came often home to our house, and always in my master's absence was doing with my dame. Wherefore, desirous that my master might know it (for they spent his goods so lavishly between them that, notwithstanding his great trade of merchandise, they had, unweeting to him, almost undone him already), I sought how I might bewray them. Which as hap would, at the time remembered afore, came to pass thus. While this gentleman was doing with my dame, my master came in—so suddenly that he had no leisure to pluck up his hose, but with them about his legs ran into a corner behind the painted cloth, and there stood (I warrant you) as still as a mouse. As soon as my master came in, his wife, according to her old wont, caught him about his neck and kissed him, and devised many means to have got him forth again. But he, being weary, sat down and called for his dinner. And when she saw there was none other remedy, she brought it him, which was a mess of potage and a piece of beef, whereas she and her franion had broke their fast with capons, hot venison, marrow bones, and all other kind of dainties.

"I, seeing this, and minding to show my master how he was ordered, got behind the cloth, and to make the man speak I all to-pawed him with my claws upon his bare legs and buttocks. And for all this, he stood still and never moved. But my master heard me and, thinking I was catching a mouse, bade my dame go help me. Who, knowing what beast was there, came to the cloth and called me away, saying, 'Come puss, come puss,' and cast me meat into the floor. But I, minding another thing, and seeing that scratching could not move him, suddenly I leaped up and caught him by the genitals with my teeth, and bote so hard that, when he had restrained more than I thought any

man could, at last he cried out, and caught me by the
neck thinking to strangle me. My master, not smelling
but hearing such a rat as was not wont to be about
such walls, came to the cloth and lift it up, and there
found this bare-arst gentleman strangling me who had
his stones in my mouth. And when I saw my master
I let go my hold, and the gentleman his. And away
I ran immediately to the place where I now dwell, and
never came there since. So that how they agreed among
them I cannot tell, nor never durst go see for fear of
my life.

*Whoredom will
be known be
it never so
warily hid.*

[10]

"Thus have I told you, my good lords, all things
that have been done and happened through me,
wherein you perceive my loyalty and obedience to all
good laws, and how shamelessly and falsely I am
accused for a transgressor. And I pray you, as you have
perceived, so certify my liege great Cammoloch (whose
life both Hagat and Heg preserve) of my behavior."

*There be false
accusers among
all kind of
creatures.*

[20]

When Grisard, Isegrim, and Pol-noir, the commissioners, had heard this declaration and request of
Mouse-slayer, they praised her much. And after that
they had commanded her, with all the cats there, to
be on St. Catherine's day next ensuing at Caithness
where, as they said, Cammoloch would hold his court,
they departed. And I, glad to have heard that I
heard, and sorry that I had not understood what was
said the other two nights before, got me to my bed
and slept a-good.

*Justices should
cherish the inno-
cents accused.*

[25]
*Travail and
watching maketh
sound sleeping.*

[30]

And the next morning, when I went out into the
garden, I heard a strange cat ask of our cat what
Mouse-slayer had done before the commissioners those
three nights. To whom our cat answered, that she had
purged herself of a crime that was laid to her charge
by Catch-rat, and declared her whole life for six years'
space. Whereof in the first two years as she said, said
she, she had five masters: a priest, a baker, a lawyer,
a broker, and a butcher; all whose privy deceits which
she had seen she declared the first night. In the next

*Mouse-slayer was
six year old.*

Cats change their
dwellings often.

[5]
Men ought to lie
with their wives.

[10]
A niggard is
neither good to
his self nor to
any other.
[15]

The Devil
delighteth to
dwell among
money.

All in this book
is nothing in
comparison of
that the cat
told before.

Gross meats
make gross wits.

[35]
Wonders are
incredible.

two years she had seven masters: a bishop, a knight, a pothecary, a goldsmith, an usurer, an alchemist, and a lord; whose cruelty, study, craft, cunning, niggishness, folly, waste, and oppression she declared the second night, wherein this doing was notable. Because the knight, having a fair lady to his wife, gave his mind so much to his book that he seldom lay with her, this cat, pitying her mistress and minding to fray him from lying alone, on a night when her master lay from her, got to his mouth and drew so his breath that she almost stifled him. A like part she played with the usurer, who, being rich and yet living miserably and feigning him poor, she got one day, while his treasure chest stood open, and hid her therein; whereof he not knowing locked her in it. And when at night he came thither again and heard one stirring there, and thinking it had been the Devil, he called the priest and many other persons to come and help him to conjure. And when in their sight he opened his chest, out leaped she and they saw what riches he had and cessed him thereafter. As for what was done and said yesternight, both of my lord Grisard's hard adventure and of Mouse-slayer's bestowing her other two last years, which is nothing in comparison of any of the other two years before, I need not tell you for you were present and heard it yourself.''

This talk, lo, I heard between these two cats. And then I got me in, and brake my fast with bread and butter, and dined at noon with common meat, which so repleted my head again and my other powers in the first digestion, that by nighttime they were as gross as ever they were before. For when I harkened at night to other two cats, which as I perceived by their gestures spake of the same matter, I understood never a word.

Lo, here have I told you all (chiefly you, my lord) a wonderful matter, and yet as incredible as it is wonderful. Notwithstanding, when I may have convenient time, I will tell you other things which these eyes of mine have seen and these ears of mine have heard, and that of mysteries so far passing this, that all which I have said now shall in comparison thereof be nothing at all to be believed. In the meanwhile, I will pray you to help to get me some money to convey me on my journey to Caithness, for I have been going thither these five years and never was able to perform my journey.

In comparison of a diamond, crystal hath no color.

When Master Ferrers had promised that he would, every man shut up his shop windows, which the foresaid talk kept open two hours longer than they should have been.

Poverty hindreth many excellent attempts.

[10]

AN EXHORTATION

I know these things will seem marvelous to many men,
that cats should understand and speak, have a governor
among themselves, and be obedient to their laws. And
were it not for the approved authority of the ecstatical
author of whom I heard it, I should myself be as   [5]
doubtful as they. But seeing I know the place and the
persons with whom he talked of these matters before
he experimented his wonderful and strange confections, I am the less doubtful of any truth therein.
Wherefore, seeing he hath in his oration proved that   [10]
cats do understand us and mark our secret doings, and
so declare them among themselves; that through help
of the medicines by him described any man may, as
he did, understand them; I would counsel all men to
take heed of wickedness, and eschew secret sins and   [15]
privy mischievous counsels, lest, to their shame, all
the world at length do know thereof. But if any man,
for doubt hereof, do put away his cat, then shall his
so doing testify his secret naughty living, which he
is more ashamed his cat should see than God and   [20]
His angels, which see, mark, and behold all men's
closest doings.

And that we may take profit by this declaration of
Master Streamer, let us so live, both openly and privily that neither our own cat, admitted to all secrets,   [25]
be able to declare aught of us to the world save what
is laudable and honest; nor the Devil's cat, which will
we or nill we seeth and writeth all our ill doings, have
ought to lay against us afore the face of God, who not
only with shame but with everlasting torment will   [30]
punish all sin and wickedness. And ever when thou
goest about anything, call to mind this proverb, *Beware*

the Cat; not to tie up thy cat till thou have done, but to see that neither thine own nor the Devil's cat (which cannot be tied up) find anything therein whereof to accuse thee to thy shame.

[5]   Thus doing, thou canst not do amiss; but shalt have such good report through the cat's declaration, that thou shalt, in recompence of Master Streamer's labor who giveth thee this warning, sing unto God this hymn of his making.

[10]

THE HYMN

Who givest wit to whales, to apes, to owls;
And kindly speech to fish, to flesh, to fowls;
And spirit to men in soul and body clean,
[15]   *To mark and know what other creatures mean;*

Which hast given grace to Gregory, no Pope,
No King, no Lord; whose treasures are their hope;
But silly priest, which like a streamer waves
[20]   *In ghostly good, despised of foolish knaves.*

Which hast, I say, given grace to him to know
The course of things above and here below,
With skill so great in languages and tongues
[25]   *As never breathed from Mithridates' lungs.*

To whom the hunter of birds, of mice and rats,
Did speak as plain as Kate that thrummeth hats;
By mean of whom is openly bewrayed
[30]   *Such things as closely were both done and said.*

To him grant, Lord, with healthy wealth and rest,
Long life to unload to us his learned breast;
With fame so great to overlive his grave,
[35]   *As none had erst, nor any after have.*

FINIS

Imprinted at London by John Allde, Anno
Domini 1570, and are to be sold by John
Arnold at the North Door of Paul's.

NOTES

1.heading T.K.: possibly Thomas Knell the younger, fl. 1560–1581 (DNB). The verses "To the Reader" were not part of Baldwin's work and are lacking in A and G. They were first added to the 1584 edition to explain why it was earlier withheld from publication (see stanza 1) and to indicate its applicability to the renewed fears of dangers from a Catholic plot in the 1580s.

1.1 *Beware the Cat*: not recorded as proverbial. When used by Skelton (*Speak Parrot*, 99) and in the *Image of Hypocrisy* (50), the phrase means merely that a bird or rat should fear a cat; but for Baldwin it means that your cat knows and will reveal your most secret doings, so conduct yourself properly (see 54.10-11).

3.heading *Love and Live*...Master: A, G, *omit* 84.

3.heading *Love and Live*: the personal motto which Baldwin placed before each of his works, perhaps with reference to Matthew 5:44–45.

3.heading John Young: probably the courtier who in 1551 attended the Marquess of Northampton on his embassy to France and who was knighted by Elizabeth during her 1574 visit to Bristol (J. G. Nichols, *Literary Remains of Edward VI* [1857], 317, 582; F. B. Williams, Jr., *Index to Dedications* [1962], 206; W. A. Shaw, *Knights of England*, 2 [1906]: 76). J. P. Collier's guess (*History of English Dramatic Poetry*, 1 [1879]: 133) that Young was a court interluder is certainly wrong, for such a person would not have been addressed as "right worshipful."

3.2-9 Master Streamer...Willot: see notes to 5.1-20.

3.14 notes: side notes, marginalia.

3.17 plow with his oxen: from Judges 14:18.

3.25 *Cure of the Great Plague:* no such work is known, but the title has topical reference because the last visitation of the mysterious sweating sickness (different from the bubonic plague) had raged in London in July of 1551, when about two thousand people died. Dr. John Caius' authoritative description, *A Book Against the Sweating Sickness,* was printed by Richard Grafton in 1552.

3.27 Margate: a coastal village in Kent, north of Dover.

4.8 G[ulielmus] B[aldwin]: the initials combined with the motto "Love and Live" identify Baldwin; but he is also named as the author in the 1569 entry in the Stationers' Register and in the 1570 *A Short Answer to Beware the Cat* (STC 664.5). J. P. Collier, *History of English Dramatic Poetry*, 1 (1831): xx, who knew only the Douce fragment and *A Short Answer,* was the first modern scholar to make the identification.

5.1 at: at 84, < > A, at the G.

5.1-20 Christmas last...Master Ferrers: George Ferrers, 1500(?)–1579 (DNB), a prominent lawyer, soldier, courtier, and poet, who later collaborated with Baldwin in writing *A Mirror for Magistrates,* was Master of the King's Pastimes during the Christmas seasons of 1551–1552 and 1552–1553. The detailed financial accounts of these festivities have been edited by Albert Feuillerat, *Documents Relating to the Revels at Court in the Time of King Edward VI and Queen Mary* (Louvain, 1914), 56–86 and 89–125, from which it is clear that 28 December 1552 is the time referred to, for only then did Ferrers have "a divine" and "an astronomer" in his train (89) and were payments made to Baldwin for properties and boat hire (142–143).

5.11-12 Master Willot. . .his Astronomer: a Thomas Willet is mentioned as sub-almoner to Edward VI (DNB s.n. Andrew Willet), but no such name occurs in the Revels Accounts.

5.11-13 Master Streamer. . .his Divine: Streamer's first name was Gregory, and he was a priest (55.19); he knew Arabic, Chaldean, Egyptian, and Greek (17.9-10); and he was the author of several books (3.25-26, 9.29, 36.4). In 1570 the humorless author of *A Short Answer to Beware the Cat* assumed that he was a real person who "many witty things writes for his country's sake"; and there was a Gregory Streamer at Oxford in 1529–1531 (C. W. Boase, *Register of the University of Oxford,* 1 [1885]: 173, 351). But his name does not appear in the Revels Accounts, no author named Streamer is recorded, no *Cure of the Great Plague* translated from Arabic or *Book of Heaven and Hell* are known, and John Day did not print any "Greek alphabets" during the reign of Edward VI. It seems clear that Streamer is a fiction, characterized by the turgid flow of his narrative.

5.22 Aesop's Crow: no such play, nor costumes appropriate to it, are recorded in the detailed Revels Accounts for this Christmas, though several literal-minded theatrical historians, with Baldwin as their authority, solemnly list "Aesop's Crow" as a play actually performed before the king. The fable concerns an ugly crow ridiculed for strutting in feathers plucked from other birds (Horace, *Epistles* 1.3.18–20); Babrius (no. 72) tells the same story of a jackdaw. A prose version, featuring a crow, appeared in Renaissance Latin editions of Aesop (T.W. Baldwin, *Shakspere's Small Latine,* 1 [1944]: 619).

5.24-25 not comical: not appropriate in a dramatic representation.

5.26 common: talk together.

6.1 ware: aware.

6.9 elephants: see Richard Sherry, *A Treatise of Schemes and Tropes,* 1550, sig. K4v.

6.14-15 swallows. . .eyes: Pliny, *Natural History,* 8.98.

6.17 kindly: suitable to its kind.

6.28 Albertus': Albertus' 84, Alberts A, G. The *Liber Aggregationis seu Liber Secretorum,* first printed in 1477, was wrongly attributed to the thirteenth-century philosopher Albertus Magnus; it went through many early editions in Latin and was translated into English (c. 1550) as *The Book of Secrets of the Virtues of Herbs, Stones, and Certain Beasts* (ed. M. R. Best and F. H. Brightman, Oxford, 1973). It is a collection of unbelievable marvels (though none of the activities of the animals listed above are mentioned) and magic formulas (such as the one quoted at 25.14-15) which the Tudors enjoyed but did not take seriously—even the English translator recommended his book as a work of entertainment rather than information.

6.35 experimenting: experiencing.

9.2 friend's house: contemporaries would recognize this as the printing shop and dwelling of the well-known publisher John Day, who occupied premises over Aldersgate from 1548 until 1553. Like Baldwin's employer Whitchurch, Day was a radical Protestant who devoted his printing almost entirely to religious works in furtherance of the Reformation.

9.5-23 Streamer's irrelevant and pompous explanations of the names of seven of the ten principal gates of London have little or no basis in fact. Aldrich, Aluredus (Alfred), and Aldgay appear to be made-up names; King Lud is a fiction of Geoffrey of Monmouth; the cripple who stole the weathercock (which was of copper, not silver) from St. Paul's Cathedral is pure fabrication, though Baldwin's story of the cripple was repeated before 1600 by Thomas Deloney in his *Thomas of Reading*, chap. 6; and in 1617 John Davies of Hereford published an epitaph "On the cripple who stole the weathercock of Paul's" in his *Wits Bedlam*, sig. L4. In 1598, John Stow (*Survey of London*, ed. C. L. Kingsford, 1 [1908]: 34) wrote of Aldersgate: "so called not of Aldrich or of elders, that is to say, ancient men, builders thereof; not of eldern trees growing there more abundantly than in other places, as some have fabled (in a book called *Beware the Cat*), but for the very antiquity of the gate itself, as being one of the first four gates of the city.... John Day, stationer, a late famous printer of many good books, in our time dwelt in this gate, and built much upon the wall of the city towards the parish church of St. Anne."

9.29 it: they G, it A, 84.

10.2 six-square bowls: six-sided bowling balls, i.e. dice.

10.3 living: clerical benefice.

10.4 baggagical: worthless.

10.13 leads: lead-covered roof.

10.13 quarters of men: the penalty for treason was to be hanged, cut down while still alive, disemboweled, and cut into quarters; the head was set on a pike on London Bridge, and the quarters were placed on various gates of the city. A priest had been quartered in July 1548; three Norfolk rebels in August 1549; and four Devonshire rebels in January 1550 (*Wriothesley's Chronicle*, Camden Society, n.s. 20 [1877]: 4, 32).

10.17 Moses: Deuteronomy 21:22-23.

10.25 Molochitus: Moloch, a heathen idol to which human sacrifices were made (Leviticus 18:21).

10.38 certain of the house: in addition to Streamer, the speakers are (1) the man from Staffordshire, who told of the cat in Kankwood forty years ago; (2) Thomas, who had been in Ireland thirty-three years ago, repeated the churl's tale of Grimalkin, had a friend who roasted a cat, told of werewolves, and later died in Newgate; (3) another, who objected to the reasonableness of Thomas' story; and (4) Master Sherry, who believed in witches and explained that the Bishop of Alexandria understood birds.

11.4 in communication of: into talk about.

11.10 kitling: kitten.

11.12 Kankwood: Cannock Chase, a royal forest in Staffordshire.

11.19 Grimalkin: also spelled Grimmalkin, Grimolochin. This is the first known occurrence of the name, probably a coinage of Baldwin's from "grey malkin," a grey female demon (see *Macbeth*, I.i.8). Leo Spitzer, *JEGP*, 43 (1944), derives "grimal kin" from "grimaud," a demon. A later political satire is titled *Grimalkin, or, the Rebel-Cat*, London, 1681. The story is a variation of Plutarch's account, in "Of the Obsolescence of Oracles" (*Moralia*, 419 B-E), of the pilot Thamus who in the time of Tiberius (14–37 A.D.) was ordered by a mysterious voice to announce, when his ship came opposite Palodes, that Great Pan was dead; he did so, and a great cry of lamentation went up from the island. Plutarch's story was quoted by Eusebius (*Praeparatio Evangelica*, 5.17) to explain the cessation of pagan oracles during the lifetime of Christ, an explanation that was widely disseminated (see Spenser's *Shepherds Calendar*, gloss to May 54).

  Baldwin's story itself became a folktale and was recorded from oral recitation in several places in England from the second half of the nineteenth century onward as Dildrum King of Cats, Molly Dixon, etc. (see Katherine M. Briggs, *A Dictionary of British Folk Tales*, Part B, 1 [1971]: 206, 294, 309). The version cited by W. E. A. Axon in *Cheshire Gleanings* (1894), 136, is verbatim from Baldwin, perhaps from Malcomson's 1868 quotation (see note to 12.8 below).

11.33 ought: owned.

12.4 that: that which.

12.8-13 Mac Murrough...Cahir Mac Art: Thomas' syntax is contorted. His meaning is that the Fitz Harrises and the prior of Tintern, the king's friends, were at war with the wild Irish, Mac Murrough and Cahir Mac Art.

12.8-14.23 Thomas' report of the Irish churl's tale is reasonably accurate in its family and place names (preserved in contemporary county Wexford records), precise in its account of the customs of the Irish, and sprinkled with enough Irish words ("coshery," "kern," "fassock") to suggest familiarity with the vocabulary of the region (see notes by the Rev. James Graves in R. Malcomson's "Notice of Beware the Cat," *Journal of the Historical and Archaeological Association of Ireland*, 3rd ser., 1[1868]: 187–192. The events are even given a date in historical time, for since Streamer mixed his potion about 11 June 1551 (27.24 and note) and since the fictional time of Patrick Apore's adventure was approximately forty years prior (11.31-32), the death of Grimalkin would supposedly have occurred in 1511.

The early records of Wexford are fragmentary, so that the principal persons named, even if they were historical, cannot be identified precisely; but the situation and the names are typical of the time. In 1336 Mac Morrough, chief of the clan Kavanagh, defeated the Englishmen of Wexford under Sir Mathew Fitz Henry; in 1525, Nicholas Fitz Henry and others, pursued by Irishmen, fled to the town of Ross, but the inhabitants closed the gates against them and they were slain (H. F. Hore, *History of Wexford*, 1[1900]: 63, 233). The priory of Tintern, founded by Welsh monks in the thirteenth century, was dissolved in 1538. The Fitz Henrys (Fitz Harrises in the text) and the Butlers were families of Anglo-Norman descent who sided with the English and carried on local warfare against the native Irish. Mac Morrough was the name or title of descendants of the ancient kings of Leinster. The historical Cahir Mac

Art Kavanagh, d. 1554 (DNB), assumed the title of Mac Murrough from 1547 to 1550. The land had been laid waste from Clonmines, on Barrow Bay near Tintern Abbey, inland to Ross (a Mac Murrough stronghold) abut fifteen miles north on the Barrow River. The fassock of Bantry lay between this area and the English town of Wexford to the east.

12.8 Mac Murrough: Mackmorro A, 84.

12.8 wild lords: native Irish leaders.

12.10 Fitz Harrises: Fizharises A, Filzharises 84.

12.12-13 Cahir Mac Art: Cayr Macart A, 84.

12.15 Wexford: Washford A, 84.

12.17 Clonmines: Climine A, 84.

12.19 coshery: a feast.

12.19 Fitz Harris: Filzberies A, Filzbeberies 84.

12.24 kern: soldier.

12.25 fassock: fassagh, wilderness area (not in OED).

12.27 Cahir Mac Art: Cayer Makart A, 84.

12.29 his country: Cahir Mac Art's.

12.33 doubting: fearing.

13.8 feres: means for lighting a fire, flint.

13.25 sod: seethed, boiled.

13.27 laps: wrappings.

14.1 and: *omit* A, 84.

14.3 flang: threw.

14.3 struck: stroke A, 84.

14.4 sight: a multitude, a great show.

14.14 started: started 84, start A.

14.18 thirty-three: xxxiiij A, 84 [a misprint or error in addition].

14.18-20 thirty-three winters past...seven years before: see introduction. The time is forty years ago at 11.31-32. See 12.24 and 14.18-19.

15.15 baggagical: worthless.

15.20 Henry VII: no other version of this anecdote has been found.

15.36 lewdly: ignorantly.

16.8m occupy: make use of.

16.9-10 in pastime, to roast a cat alive: as part of the midsummer festivities at Paris in 1572, a fox and live cats were suspended in a bag over a bonfire (James M. Osborn, *Young Philip*

Sidney [New Haven, 1972], 43). See Robert Darnton, *The Great Cat Massacre* (1984), chap. 2, especially 83–85, 89–96. Bear baiting and cock fighting were also popular spectator sports, as bull fighting and prize fighting are today.

16.13 quick: live.

16.16 sort: great number.

16.17 scrat: scratched.

16.21m Master Sherry: probably Richard Sherry, an Oxford M.A. and former headmaster of Magdalen College School, whose translation of J. Brentius' *Exposition upon the Sixth Chapter of St. John* (the miracles of the loaves and fishes and of Christ walking upon the water) was printed by John Day on 9 April 1550 and whose *Treatise of Schemes and Tropes* was printed by Day in December 1550, only a few months before June 1551, the supposed date of the events told to Streamer in Day's printing house.

16.25 hagat: hag or heg, a witch (see 36.30-31).

16.28 a cat hath nine lives: Tilley W 6520 (1546).

16.32 Pythonesses: equated with the witch of Endor (Chaucer, *Friar's Tale*, III, 1510) in 1 Samuel 28:7–15. The Geneva Version sidenote explains that the form of Samuel appeared to Saul, "To his imagination, albeit was Satan, who to blind his eyes took upon him the form of Samuel."

16.36 telchines: metal-working magicians of Rhodes who kill with a glance (Ovid, *Metamorphoses*, 7.365; Strabo, 14.2.7).

17.8-9 *Sapiens*...Socrates: for the wise hide their knowledge. Socrates is wise because he knows he has no wisdom (*Apology* 21).

17.10 Calde: Chaldean, the biblical Aramaic.

17.14 Nichodem: Nicodemus (John 3:3–4). "Jesus said, 'Except a man be born again, he cannot see the kingdom of God.' Nicodemus asked, 'How can a man be born which is old? Can he enter into his mother's womb again, and be born?' "

17.14-16m Popish conjurer...Transubstantiationers: Transubstantiation, the Roman Catholic doctrine that the bread and wine of the sacrament are changed into Christ's body and blood, "the appearance alone of the bread and wine remaining," was adopted as an official article of faith by the fourth Lateran council in 1215 and reaffirmed by the Council of Trent. It was denied by the Reformers. Cf. 38.17-20, 38.28-29, and introduction.

17.25 candle: "When thou wilt that they which be in a place seem without heads, take smart brimstone, with oil, and put it in a lamp and make light with it, and put it in the midst of men, and thou shalt see a marvellous thing" (Albertus Magnus, *Book of Secrets*, ed. Best and Brightman, 89–90).

17.35–19.31 For in Ireland...witches...red swine...wolves: The Rev. James Graves (in Malcomson, note to 12.8-14.23 above, p. 192) pointed out that the werewolf story was from Giraldus Cambrensis, but did not note that the other anecdotes are also from the same source. Baldwin must have used a manuscript, because the *Topographia Hibernica* was not printed until 1603 in William Camden's *Anglica, Normannica, Hibernica, Cambrica, a Veteribus Scripta.* An abbreviated paraphrase of 2.19 (721–724), "De lupo cum sacerdote loquente," follows.

> About three years before the coming of Prince John into Ireland [i.e. 1182], a priest on a journey spent the night in a forest near Meath. A wolf came up to him and explained that by the curse of St. Natalis a man and woman from Ossory had been turned into wolves, who, if they survived seven years, could resume their human shapes, but then two others must take their places. He said his companion was mortally ill and asked the priest to administer the last rites to her. He led the priest to a tree where an old she-wolf lay groaning. The wolf pulled the skin from her head and the priest saw she was an old woman; he administered the last rites, and the wolf thanked him. Two years later the bishop of Meath asked me [Giraldus] what he should do about the matter, and I advised him to send an account of it to the pope attested under his seal, which he did. It must be believed that as divine nature for the salvation of the world assumed human nature, so in this case God, to show his power by no less a miracle, caused human nature to assume that of a wolf. Augustine, in his *City of God* 18.18, wrote of similar transformations, that when he was in Italy he heard of stablewomen, who had learned evil arts, who fed travelers something in cheese that transformed them into beasts and made them bear burdens. And also in our own time I have seen persons by magical arts turn things into red swine, which they sold, but which disappeared as soon as they crossed water. Likewise certain old women in Wales, Ireland, and Scotland take the shape of a hare. But I agree with Augustine (*City of God*, 18.18) that evil men cannot really change their natures; though those whom God created can appear to be transformed, the senses of men being deceived by illusion, drawn by some magical incantation to see false and fictitious forms. Of that change of the bread into the body of Christ, truly substantial because while the appearance remains the same the substance is changed, I do not wish to treat because its comprehension is beyond human understanding.

Baldwin has changed the order of the anecdotes (first, the red swine; second, the werewolves; and third, the witch and hermit), but the essential details are from Giraldus, even the following discussion of how men's sights are deceived. Baldwin was probably led to the passage by the reference to transubstantiation with which Giraldus concludes, and indeed the fundamental fictional construct of *Beware the Cat*, that belief in the physical efficacy of the mass is as absurd as belief in animals having power of speech, may have had its beginning here.

18.1-2 act . . . Ireland . . . red swine: the story of the red swine is from Giraldus, above; no such Irish enactment existed.

18.19 Saint Patrick: in the printed text of Giraldus, St. Natalis delivered the curse. Patrick may have appeared in the manuscript Baldwin had access to, but if so the reference would be to the eleventh-century Patrick, Bishop of Dublin (see J. J. O'Meara, *The First Version of the Topography of Ireland* [Dundalk, 1951], 114–116).

18.33-34 hermit...St. Augustine: *City of God* 18.18 quoted by Giraldus, above, about stable-women and travelers.

19.8 Naaman's: in 2 Kings 5, Elisha caused Naaman's leprosy to be visited upon his own avaricious servant Gehazi and upon that man's descendants forever.

23.7-8 my Lord's chapel: probably a reference to a company of choristers kept by some great nobleman; the allusion could not be to the Chapel Royal, which was headed by a dean.

23.8 scaffold: stage, platform.

23.9-10 diatesseron, diapente, diapason: musical intervals of a fourth, a fifth, and an octave respectively.

23.11 bear: in the Tudor sport of bear baiting, a chained bear was set upon by a pack of mastiffs.

23.11 let slip: unleashed.

23.15 double diapason: probably two-part harmony of base and treble (not in OED).

23.20 closely: secretly.

23.23 becks: gestures of salutation or respect.

24.3 incontinently: immediately.

24.17 by and by: at once.

24.25 Albertus Magnus' works: see note to 6.28. Streamer used the Latin text of *Liber Secretorum de Virtutibus Herbarum, Lapidum et Animalium,* which reads: "Si tu vis intelligere voces avium: tunc associa tecum duos socios in quinto kalendas Novembris [28 October, the day of Saints Simon and Judas], et tunc vade in quoddam nemus cum canibus quasi ad venandum et illam bestiam quam primo inveneris defer tecum ad domum et prepara cum corde vulpis et statim intelliges voces avium vel bestiarum. Et si tu vis ut aliquis intelligat, oscula eum et intelliget similiter" (London, c. 1486, sig. E2). He translated the passage at 17.21-27 in wording different from that of the printed English version (see *Book of Secrets,* ed. Best and Brightman, 98–99).

24.35 other of: others, with A, other 84.

24.37-25.4 Phoebus...Lucifer: a description of sunrise in pompously inflated style, which Baldwin underscores in his sidenote, "the resurrection of the sun." Cf. Chaucer, *Franklin's Tale,* V, 1016–1018; Cervantes, *Don Quixote,* I, ii, "Apenas había el rubicundo Apolo...."

25.1 Thetis: the sea personified.

25.3 Hera's dry lap: Streamer apparently means the earth, though Hera, as wife of Zeus, is queen of the heavens, and fruitful rather than dry (barren).

25.4 advouterer: adulterer.

25.4 Lucifer: the light bearer, the morning star (Venus).

25.5 Europa: Europe.

25.6 Mile-End steeple: located approximately a mile outside Aldgate, the eastern gate of London; Aldersgate, where Streamer is, lies to the north-west of Aldgate.

25.20 kissest: kissed A, kistest 84.

25.30 St. Jude's Day: 28 October—Streamer prepared his philter about 11 June (27.24).

25.32 hedgehog: urchin, a spiny nocturnal quadruped. See 26.15 and frontispiece to text.

25.33m planetical: planetary (no association seems to exist between the hedgehog and any planet).

25.36 subtile: rarefy.

26.1 St. John's Wood: northwest of Aldersgate, outside the city walls, near Islington.

26.6 case: skin.

26.7 slip: leash, used as a whip.

26.15 urchin: hedgehog. Later associated with fairies by Reginald Scot, Nashe, and Shakespeare, because of magical qualities.

26.17 in the game: to the sport (of hunting). Not found elsewhere is the superstition that naming a hedgehog brings bad luck to hunters.

26.26 crabs: crabapples.

26.27m Albertus saith: not in the *Liber Secretorum*.

26.27-28 and 26.36 Shavol...Javol...: not in the *Liber Secretorum*.

26.37 mess: food for a meal.

27.1 Thomas: the member of the company of the preceding evening who had repeated the story of the death of Grimalkin (see note to 10.38).

27.8 farced: stuffed.

27.10-11 departed with his cat: Streamer forgets that in the preceding sentence he had said the company had eaten it up "every morsel."

27.12-14 Doctor Nicholas...anatomy: this should be a well-known contemporary surgeon, but no such name appears in Sidney Young's *Annals of the Barber-Surgeons of London* (1890). Nicholas of Salerno, whose *Antidotarium* (c. 1140) was the first medical work to be printed (Venice, 1471), wrote on physic rather than anatomy.

27.15-16 Mellisophillos: Sir Thomas Elyot, in his 1538 *Dictionary*, likens melissa to balm and melissophyllum to smallage.

27.19m Par...est. gib.: "The first number even, the last uneven. gib." "gib" may be an abbreviation for a personal name.

27.19 limbec: alembic, chemical still.

27.21 pottle: half a gallon.

27.23 *solstitium estivale:* the summer solstice, 21 June (11 June Old Style), in the year 1551 (see note to 37.31).

27.23-25m Omne...Zoroast: "Zoroaster says everything should be done in accordance with the proper planet."

27.26–31.8 Mercury...could: Albertus Magnus, in whose *Liber Secretorum* Streamer had found the formula by which the voices of animals might be understood, also included a *Discourse of the Nature and Qualities of the Seven Planets* (see the edition by Best and Brightman, 61–73), in which he noted that "every true act must be done under his planet; and it is better if it be done in the proper day of the planet, and in his own proper hour, as for an example...under Mercury, loss, debt, fear." Albertus gave elaborate instructions for finding the hour when each planet was dominant on each day of the week. Streamer, for all his ostentatious parade of the names of planets and their hours, had only partially read Albertus' instructions and certainly did not understand them.

In the first place, the unequal planetary hours are usually different in length from the equal solar hours. A solar day consists of twenty-four equal sixty-minute hours from midnight to noon and noon to midnight. A planetary day consists of twelve hours from sunrise to sunset, and a planetary night of twelve hours from sunset to sunrise; therefore the lengths of the planetary hours of the day and the night differ from one another in length and vary according to the season of the year—only at the equinoxes are the planetary hours of the day and night of equal length and equal to the solar hours. Streamer reported that he undertook his experiment at the time of the summer solstice, and by coincidence Albertus explained the planetary hours with an example fitting that season, when the sun rises at four in the morning and sets sixteen hours later at eight in the evening, so that the twelve hours of the planetary day are each eighty minutes in length, and the twelve hours of the planetary night are each forty minutes in length. But Streamer pays no attention to the unequal planetary hours and gives all his time references in terms of equal solar or clock hours, which he improperly assumes to be the same as planetary hours.

In the second place, as Albertus explains, the seven planets, beginning with the one at the greatest distance from the earth, rotate in the order Saturn, Jupiter, Mars, Sun, Venus, Mercury, and Moon. The dominion of each planet begins at sunrise on the appropriate day of the week and becomes dominant again on the eighth hour of the day and the third and tenth hour of the night. A different planet begins its dominance at sunrise on each day of the week—on Sunday the Sun is dominant during the first hour of the day, on Monday the Moon, on Tuesday Mars, on Wednesday Mercury, on Thursday Jupiter, on Friday Venus, and on Saturday Saturn. But Streamer makes no reference to the day of the week, does not take into account the season of the year, and even partly confuses the order of succession of his planets.

Streamer begins (27.24) by saying that at the summer solstice Mercury was dominant at the solar time of 10:00 a.m., which is impossible because at that season the planetary hour would begin at 10:40 rather than at 10:00 solar time. But he throughout ignorantly assumes that planetary time is the same as solar time. He goes on to say (28.12-13) that the Sun began its dominance at noon. But if Mercury was dominant at ten, Saturn would become dominant two hours later, which is the reason for Baldwin's sidenote pointing out that "Master Streamer varieth from the astronomers in his planet hours."

After dinner at noon Streamer slept an hour, then he prepared a poultice and, "when Saturn's dry hour of dominion approached" (29.7-8—if the Sun was dominant at noon, Saturn would become dominant four hours later), applied it to his ears. The Sun's dominion began again, he said, at six that night (29.25); but if the Sun was dominant at noon, it would not become dominant again until the second hour of the night, which would be eight o'clock according to Streamer's improper method of equating solar and planetary time. Two hours after (29.27-28), Mercury's reign approached—which is correct, because Mercury comes second after the sun. Streamer then went to his chamber "past nine of the clock" when "the hour of Saturnus' cold dominion approached" (30.34-35). This calculation is again correct because Saturn is fourth in planetary order after the sun (which would dominate before 10:00 p.m., according to Streamer's method of figuring). And finally, as Jupiter's hour of dominion approached (31.4-5), he took the pads from his ears and found his hearing had been rendered marvellously acute. This would be slightly more than an hour before midnight. What is made clear by Streamer's references to the hours of planetary dominance is that he knew a few terms, but was entirely confused about both astronomical and astrological systems. He attempts to parade his learning, but instead reveals his ignorance.

27.27m *Omne...Trismeg.:* Everything as a whole is totally evil. [Hermes] Trismeg [istus].

27.28 milt: spleen.

27.29 lights: lungs.

27.35m Deus...gaudet: "Heaven delights in an uneven number." ("Numero deus impare gaudet," Virgil, *Eclogues,* 8.75).

28.1 stones: testicles.

28.2m Dextra...sinistris: "The good parts from the right side are truly harmful to the good parts from the left."

28.7 it in: in A, et in 84.

28.7m Calor...distillationis: "The heat of the sun is the fire for alchemical distillation."

28.10 galls: gall-bladders.

28.18m intelligible: providing understanding (not in OED).

28.24 gear: stuff.

28.29m noodle: back of the head.

28.29-30 nuke memorative: the "nuke" is the nape of the neck, and the seat of memory was supposed to be in the back part of the brain.

29.4 lowache: lovage, an umbelliferous herb (Ligusticum); lowachtsie A, lowache 84.

29.6-7 pillows: pads.

29.14 pannicle: membrane.

29.15 *dura mater:* membrane protecting the brain.

29.15 oppilations: obstructions.

29.15 ingrossing: thickening.

29.17 gargaristical: like a gargle (not in OED).

29.19 sod: seethed, broiled (see 13.25).

29.23 incorpored: incorporated, combined in one mass.

29.24 trochisks: lozenges.

29.29 stilled: distilled.

29.33 reins: kidneys.

29.34 chine bone: jaw bone.

29.34 Alkakengi: red winter cherry or nightshade; alka kghi A, Alkakengy 84.

30.4 shrewd: malicious.

30.4 crack-rope: a person destined to be hanged.

30.6 presciencial: foreseeing (a word apparently coined by Streamer). The episode is adapted from *Tales and Quick Answers* (c. 1535, chap. 91), "Of the scoffer that made a man a soothsayer":

"There was a merry scoffing fellow on a time the which took on him to teach a man to be a soothsayer. When they were agreed what he should have for his labor, the scoffer said to the man, 'Hold! Eat this round pellet and I warrant thou shalt be a soothsayer.' The man took and put it in his mouth and began to champ thereon, but it savored so ill that he spit it out forthwith and said, 'Fie, this pellet that thou givest me to eat savoreth all of a turd.' 'Thou sayest truth,' quod the scoffer, 'now thou are a *sooth*sayer and therefore pay me my money'."

The jest appears in Anatole de Montaiglon and Gaston Reynaud, *Recueil des fabliaux des XIIIe et XIVe siècles*, 3 (Paris, 1872–1890): 46–48; Poggio Bracciolini, *Facetiae*, 1451, No. 106 (107); *Howleglas*, c. 1528, chap. 23; and Andrew Borde, *Scoggin's Jests*, before 1549, No. 30.

30.13 spattle: spatter, splash.

30.21 Isegrim: the wolf in *Reynard the Fox*, but here a cat; see 37.12, 47.8.

31.5 appropinquation: approach (Streamer's coinage from "appropinquatio").

31.9 rime: rim, membrane.

31.18 'fined films: refined membranes.

31.20-21 harmony of the moving of the spheres: the music, unperceivable by human ears, made by the revolution of the spheres which carry the planets and fixed stars.

31.32 cataracts: waterspouts.

31.33 brising: crushing; brising 84, rising A.

31.34 diapason: harmony (see note to 23.10).

31.37 Chaucer's House of Fame: in II, 711–852, Chaucer indulges in a humorous fantasy in which he dreams that an eagle carries him high in the heavens to the House of Fame where, since light things naturally move upward, every speech or noise made anywhere on earth, even the squeak of a mouse, is heard greatly magnified.

32.2 obliquation: bending aside (Streamer's Latin corruption).

32.8 shrewd: shrewish.

32.9 St. Albans: a town twenty-one miles north of London.

32.11m groveth: comes into existence.

32.14 rousing: rising from cover, rushing.

32.16 scrabbling: scrabbling 84, scrapling A.

32.17 trulling: trolling, rolling.

32.17 curling: gurgling, rumbling.

32.18 chirking: chirping.

32.18 shriking: shrieking.

32.19 routing: snoring.

32.20 fizzling: breaking wind without noise.

32.22 springling: springing, causing to rise.

32.27 pannicles: membranes (see 29.14).

32.30 nearer: nearer 84, never A.

32.35 St. Botolph's: the church of St. Botolph's is about a mile east of Aldersgate.

32.36 body: body 84, lady A.

33.11m Fertilitas...nocus: "Fertility is harmful to itself."

33.26 by that: by the time that.

35.1-14 Streamer's ostentatiously learned description of moonrise (cf. his description of sunrise at 24.37-25.10).

35.4 reverberation: reflection.

35.4 Thetis: see note to 25.1.

35.5 spring: spring tide, when the high-water level reaches its maximum after the full moon.

35.7 neap: neap tide, after the first and third quarters of the moon when the water level is lowest.

35.8 rades: radiations, rays (not in OED).

35.12 upon: upon 84, after A.

35.17-36.6 Streamer reverses Ptolemaic astronomical theories with somewhat less success than Copernicus, who had not yet been heard of in England.

35.22 element: air.

35.22 opposition of: reflection from.

35.24 crystalline heaven: Streamer confuses this with the firmament, the sphere of the fixed stars. In Ptolemaic astronomy, the crystalline heaven is a sphere supposed to exist between the primum mobile and the firmament by which the precession of the equinoxes was accounted for.

35.32 like-nightical: Streamer's literal Englishing of "equinoctial" (not in OED).

36.2 cast: reflect.

36.2-3 roundness and egg-form of the firmament: See *The Kalender of Shepherdes* (1506), ed. H. O. Sommer, 3 (1892): 122.8, 123.26–27: "...the worlde is rounde lyke an aple...The elementis whiche be in it composed, is closed within the first heuen lyke as the yowlke of an egge is closed within the whyte of the egge."

36.15 'beisance: beshiens A, beysance 84.

36.30-31 Hagat and Heg: see 16.25.

36.32 Alhabor: the dog star Sirius; *Kalender of Shepherdes*, 3(1892): 136, 22–23.

37.11-12 greffier: clerk.

37.12 Grisard: grayed, grizzled.

37.12 Isegrim: see note to 30.22.

37.13 Pol-noir: black head.

37.26 strange: unfamiliar.

37.27 mate: make A, 84.

37.29–30 Stony Stratford is nearest to London in Buckinghamshire; Stratford on Avon is in Warwickshire, and the river Tyne is in Northumberland.

37.31-33 this was in the time when preachers had leave to speak against the Mass, but it [the Mass] was not forbidden till half a year after: neither the government nor the church officially encouraged attacks on the Mass, but they were condoned. The number of pulpit attacks is unrecorded, but in 1547 five books and pamphlets were published against the Mass, in 1548 twenty-three, and in 1549 three. The first Edwardian Act of Uniformity (2 & 3 Edw. VI, c. 1, 1549), which abolished the Latin Mass and established the English Communion Service, passed both Houses of Parliament by 21 January, received the royal assent on 14 March, but was not ordered into effect nationally until Whitsunday (9 June) 1549—though some parishes in London and elsewhere in England used the new Communion Service from early March onwards.

   This passage provides us with a bridge from fictional to historical time, for the first adventure narrated by Mouse-slayer occurred shortly before Whitsunday 1549 (reiterated at 39.19), and her last adventure "at Whitsuntide past"(49.38-50.1) two years later (52.23-24), which would be 17 May 1551. Mouse-slayer's other time references are general (40.2, 40.9, 46.4-6, 49.38), but they are clearly intended to chronicle the happenings of the past two years of her life.

38.17 posed you: the Reformers were shocked at the ignorance of some of the clergy. Bishop Hooper, on a visitation in 1551, found that half the clergy he examined could not repeat the Ten Commandments, and more than a tenth did not know where the Lord's Prayer appeared in the Bible (A. G. Dickens, *The English Reformation* [1964], 243).

38.24m true coal: genuine (not in OED).

38.27 God refuseth no sinners that will repent: the Protestant emphasis on election opposed the Catholic belief that confession, contrition, and penance could reduce divine punishment for sin, as in the popular stories of Robert the Devil and Mary of Nimengen, grievous sinners who repented and were saved.

38.32 souls may be brought out of Purgatory: Masses for the dead were supposed to reduce their time in Purgatory, illustrated in the popular poem *The Life of St. Gregory's Mother,* c. 1500, in which a murderess, even though she had not confessed, was released from Purgatory by the saying of a trental of Masses. The chantries, established for the saying of Masses for the dead, were dissolved by act of Edward's first Parliament (1 Edw. VI, c. 14, 1547).

38.37 by and by: immediately.

39.2m Veritas. . . angulos: "Truth seeks corners," an ironic comment on the priest shutting the door for secrecy.

39.3 revised: revested, arrayed.

39.4 porteous: portas, a portable breviary.

39.5 elevation: lifting up the Host for adoration.

39.14 forbidden them to say. . . Mass: see note to 37.31-32.

39.23 magistical: Streamer's coinage for "skilled in magic."

40.10 This woman: a character much like the procuress Celestina in *Calisto y Melibea,* part of which was translated into English about 1525.

40.24 gage: pawn.

41.10-46.3 This is the widely disseminated story of the weeping bitch, first found in the twelfth-century *Disciplina Clericalis* of Petrus Alphonsi; but, as Holden pointed out, Baldwin's immediate source is "The Fables of Alfonce," No. 11, in William Caxton's *Fables of Aesop* (1483), where "chienne" (bitch) is translated "cat":

> A nobleman was sometime which had a wife much chaste and was wonder fair. This nobleman would have gone on pilgrimage to Rome and left his wife at home because that he knew her for a chaste and a good woman. It happed on a day as she went into the town, a fair young man was esprised of her love, and took on him hardiness and required her of love, and promised to her many great gifts. But she, which was good, had lever die than to consent her thereto; wherefore the young man died almost for sorrow, to the which fellow came an old woman which demanded of him the cause of his sickness. And the young man manifested or discovered unto her all his courage and heart, asking help and counsel of her. And the old woman, wily and malicious, said to him: "Be thou glad and joyous, and take good courage; for well I shall do and bring about thy fate, in so much that thou shalt have thy will fulfilled."
>
> And after this the old bawd went to her house, and made a little cat which she had at home to fast three days one after another. And after she took some bread with a great deal or quantity of mustard upon it, and gave it to this young

cat for to eat it. And when the cat smelled it, she began to weep and cry. And the old woman or bawd went unto the house of the said young woman, and bare her little cat with her, the which young and good woman received and welcomed her much honestly, because that all the world held her for a holy woman. And as they were talking together, the young woman had pity of the cat which wept and demanded of the old woman what the cat ailed. And the old woman said to her, "Aha, my fair daughter and my fair friend, renew not my sorrow." And saying these words she began to weep and said, "My friend, for no good I will tell the cause why my cat weepeth." And then the young woman said to her, "My good mother, I pray you that ye will tell me the cause why and wherefor your cat weepeth." And then the old woman said to her, "My friend, I will well if thou wilt swear that thou shalt never rehearse it to nobody." To the which promise the good and true young woman accorded herself, supposing that it had been all good, and said, "I will well."

And then the old woman said to her in this manner: "My friend, this same cat which thou seest yonder was my daughter, the which was wonder fair, gracious and chaste, which a young man loved much and was so much esprised of her love that because that she refused him, he died for her love, wherefore the gods having pity on him have turned my daughter into this cat." And the young woman, which supposed that the old woman had said truth, said to her in this manner: "Alas, my fair mother, I ne wot what I shall do, for such a case might well hap to me. For in this town is a young man which dieth almost for the love of me, but for love of my husband, to whom I ought to keep chastity, I have not will grant him. Nevertheless, I shall do that that thou shalt counsel to me." And then the old woman said to her, "My friend, have thou pity on him as soon as thou mayest, so that it befall not to thee like as it did to my daughter." The young woman then answered to her and said, "If he require me any more, I shall accord me with him; and if he require me no more, yet shall I proffer me to him; and to the end that I offend not the gods, I shall do and accomplish it as soon as I may."

The old woman then took leave of her and went forthwith to the young man. And to him she rehearsed and told all these tidings, whereof his heart was filled with joy, the which anon went toward the young woman and with her he fulfilled his will. And thus ye may know the evils which been done by bawds and old harlots, that would to god that they were all brent.

41.17m Quid...fames: "To what dost thou not drive the hearts of men, O accursed hunger for gold" (Virgil, *Aeneid*, 3.56-57).

41.23 brake: disclosed.

41.29-30 against she should come: in preparation for her arrival.

41.34 neeze: sneeze.

41.37m glorious: vain.

42.1 gossips': friends'.

42.7 brast: burst.

42.33 honesty: chastity.

43.1 shrewd: sharp.

43.3 boot: remedy.

43.6 forpined: wasted away.

43.37 corse: corpse.

44.12-13 silly ghost: innocent spirit.

44.26 favor: face.

44.31 G. S.: the initials of the reporter, Gregory Streamer.

44.35 heaviness: sadness.

45.10-11 not make any conscience to save: not allow scruples to prevent saving.

45.16m communication: conversation—Evil speakings corrupt good manners, 1 Corinthians 15:33 (Geneva version).

45.24 quick: live.

45.27 crope: crept.

45.30-31 all to-bescrat: thoroughly scratched.

45.34 pounced: bruised, scratched.

46.8 concupiscential: lustful.

46.14 kitlings: kittens.

46.23 reremouse: bat.

46.34 ten: ten 84, two A.

47.3 savory: the herb satureia, considered an aphrodisiac by Ovid (*Ars Amatoria* 2.415) and Martial (3.75.4).

47.24 Corleonis: a fixed star in the constellation Leo.

47.25 goblins' hour: the superstition is as old as the fourth century A.D. Cf. *Hamlet* 1.1.152.

47.33 unhappy turns: reprehensible actions.

48.27 fet: fetched.

48.36m mo: more.

49.5 hawsoning: exorcizing.

49.15 all to-rayed: entirely befouled.

49.18 madly: stupefied with fear.

50.10 bewray: expose.

50.14 hose: breeches.

50.15 painted cloth: tapestry used as wall covering.

50.23 franion: paramour.

50.23m: should be "sine Cerere et Libero friget Venus" ("without Ceres and Bacchus, Venus is frigid"), Terence, *Eunuchus*, 732.

50.26-27 how he was ordered: in what group he belonged (i.e., with cuckolds).

50.37 bote: bit.

51.6 stones: testicles.

51.23 St. Catherine's Day. . .Caithness: November 25th, in the northernmost county in Scotland, used in this sentence for its alliterative effect.

52.3-4 niggishness: stinginess; niggishness 84, niggardness A.

52.20 cessed: taxed.

52.35 Lo: Lo 84, So A.

52.35 my lord: Master Ferrers.

53.10 shop windows: eyelids.

54.6 place: the printing house of John Day (Baldwin was himself a printer).

54.8 experimented: experienced.

54.19 naughty: wicked.

54.22 closest: most secret.

54.28 nill we: will we not.

55.17 Gregory: Streamer's first name; the last Pope Gregory, the XIIth, was deposed in 1409.

55.25 Mithridates: Mithridates, who ruled most of Asia Minor, was famed for his knowledge of twenty-two languages.

55.28 thrummeth: decorates with fringes.

THE BEGINNINGS OF THE ENGLISH NOVEL

Appendix 1: A History of
Longer Fictional Prose Narratives
in English to 1558

In western literature, the art of fictional narrative was brought to its earliest peak of perfection in the *Iliad* and *Odyssey,* composed in the eighth and seventh centuries B.C. Not until the third century A.D., however, do we get prose texts of the Greek romances. In Latin, we have the works of Virgil and Ovid and a number of other narrative poets before or at the beginning of the Christian era. The only Roman works of prose fiction are the fragmentary *Satyricon* of Petronius and the *Golden Ass* of Apuleius, composed in the first and second centuries A.D. Surviving from the England of Anglo-Saxon times, we have the heroic poem *Beowulf* and a few other verse narratives of medium length, but only a single, imperfectly preserved work of prose fiction, *Apollonius of Tyre*—which is not an original composition, but a translation of a continental Latin work. Indeed, for over a thousand years, from the coming of the Angles and Saxons in the fifth century until the middle of the sixteenth, no original work of prose fiction of more than short-story length was preserved in English.

1. Celtic Prose Fiction

Though no early original prose fiction written in English survived, some exists in the other languages—Celtic, Norman-French, and Latin—that were written in ancient Britain and Ireland. The Celts, who occupied Britain and Ireland from about the sixth century B.C. onward, had no writing, and so no recorded literature or history. Despite the elaborate system devised by the Druids for the oral transmission and preservation of knowledge, the Celts' own memory of their past did not endure. When they acquired Latin letters (in approximately the fifth century A.D.) and began to write down the heroic stories of their own past (possibly as early as the eighth or ninth centuries, although the earliest extant Irish prose literary manuscripts are of the twelfth century), their recollections of earlier people and events, hazy and distorted as they were, did not extend earlier than the fifth century A.D.[1]

The Celts of Ireland, unlike the Celts in England, were not conquered by the Romans and remained undisturbed until the Viking raids of the ninth century. They were a conservative people who probably maintained their culture unchanged for centuries. Their form for narrative was the saga, a prose tale with the more important or more emotional parts of the dialogue or comment in verse. This may also have been the pattern of the earliest Indo-European kind of formal narrative, for similar combinations of prose and verse are found among the earliest Sanskrit writings of India.[2] The Irish story tellers, or *filid,* who handed on their tales orally until the eighth century or later, classified their narratives by subject matter, though modern scholars group them into cycles, of which they distinguish four: the Mythological, the Ulster, the Fenian, and the Cycle of Kings. The first tells tales of the gods; the last is partly historical; and the middle two give us perhaps our earliest prose fiction in any European vernacular other than Greek and Latin. They are wildly imaginative stories about the supernatural and supermen; the tales have no regard for probability, and fantasy has complete ascendancy over fact.

The longest and most well-known is the Ulster Cycle *Táin bó Cualnge*, or *Cattle Raid of Cooley*, preserved in differing versions in three manuscripts ranging in date from the beginning of the twelfth to the end of the fourteenth century.[3] It is a pagan story in which no trace of Christianity appears; the social setting is an aristocracy of chariot-driving warriors similar to those Caesar met when he invaded Britain in the first century B.C. It narrates the mighty deeds of the hero Cu Chulainn, champion of King Conchobor of Ulster, against the warriors of Medhbh, queen of Connaught (the names are not historical), and culminates in Cu Chulainn's four-day fight with Fer Diad, his foster brother, whom he is forced to kill. Among the preliminary tales is the tragic account of Derdriu, the earliest Irish love story.

Another type of early Irish story is the immram, or fabulous voyage, the oldest of which, *The Voyage of Mael Dúin*, became the basis of the tenth-century Latin *Navigatio Sancti Brendani* (over seventeen thousand words), in which form it was widely disseminated in the Middle Ages.[4] The Irish marvels are attached to an historical person—St. Brendan, abbot of Clonfert (d. 577)—who is said to have sailed forth with seventeen fellow monks to find the land of promise of the saints. They wander for seven years and visit many marvels: the island paradise of birds (who are fallen angels), a huge fish which they mistake for an island, and a volcano at the entrance to hell near which they see Judas Iscariot being tortured by devils. They finally reach the land of promise, where it is always daylight and eternal summer; but they cannot cross the river which separates it from the true paradise, and they return to their monastery. The story attracted the imaginations of explorers, some of whom as late as the eighteenth century made voyages in search of St. Brendan's land of promise.

The Welsh prose tales, preserved in manuscripts of the fourteenth century and after, are later in origin than the Irish. The main collection is the so-called *Mabinogion*,[5] eleven separate tales, the last three of which tell the same stories as the twelfth-century French romances *Yvain*, *Perceval*, and *Erec* by Chrétien de Troyes. The longest, *Culhwch and Olwen* (only a little over seventeen thousand words), tells how Culhwch, with the aid of King Arthur (his earliest appearance in Celtic literature), various warriors with supernatural powers, and the oldest animals in the world (whose speech is understood by Gwrhyr, Interpreter of Tongues), performs seemingly impossible tasks, kills the giant Ysbaddaden, and marries Olwen. The story is notable for its grotesque, bombastic, and imaginative language, as in the description of Culhwch's battleaxe, which was "the forearm's length of a full-grown man from ridge to edge: it would draw blood from the wind; it would be swifter than the swiftest dewdrop from the stalk to the ground, when the dew would be heaviest in the month of June"(97). These Irish and Welsh tales were, until they were translated into English in the nineteenth century, known only to native Celtic speakers, though some of their eerie strangeness reappears in the work of William Baldwin, who was of Welsh descent and may have visited Ireland.

2. Anglo-Norman Prose Fiction

During the first four centuries of the Christian era, England was governed as a Roman province. When the Romans withdrew, the Saxons came, established their language and political rule, and drove the native Celtic-speaking peoples into Cornwall, Wales, and Scotland. After the Saxons came the Danes and then the Normans. With the Norman Conquest, the language of the ruling class in Britain became French for some three centuries, so that most of the literature produced during that period was written in Norman French. Though the Normans in England produced a fairly voluminous literature of considerable merit, their longer fictional narratives were all in verse. We have one exception, the early fourteenth-century *Fouke Fitz Warine* which is not an original composition but a prose reworking of a late thirteenth-century Anglo-Norman poem, the text of which is now lost.[6] It is a family romance telling the ancestry of the Fitz Warines, the rebellion of Fouke III against King John, his outlawry, and his restoration to favor. The author of the original had an accurate acquaintance with the topography of the borders of Wales and some knowledge of history (Fouke III and his brothers *were* outlawed by King John in 1201 and pardoned in 1203); but most of the episodes are either entirely imaginary or drawn from earlier French metrical romances such as *Renaud de Montauban* and *Huon de Bordeaux* (later prose versions of both of these were afterwards translated into English by Caxton and Lord Berners).

The first third of the story deals with the ancestors of Fouke Fitz Warine and includes the romantic episode of the maid Marioun who admits her lover, Ernalt de Lyls, to the castle of Dynan (the present Ludlow castle). The latter part deals with Fouke III who, with his four brothers, was brought up with the sons of King Henry II. This narrative contains a multitude of incidents. Fouke and his brothers renounce their homage to the king and live as outlaws in the forest of Bradene, where they rob the king's men, but no others, and reverse the shoes of their horses to confuse their pursuers. They meet the mariner Mador and have many adventures at sea, including the rescue of Ydoyne, daughter of the duke of Carthage, from a dragon. King John sends Sir James to capture the brothers, but Fouke kills him, disguises himself in his arms, and presents the body of Sir James to the king as that of Fouke himself. This accomplished story is all the better for its slight thread of history being interwoven with numerous strands of romance. Many of the motifs were old (the reversal of the horses' shoes was a trick played by Cacus in the *Aeneid*, and others became the foundation of later popular stories. The earliest reference to Robin Hood pairs him with Randolph, Earl of Chester (Fouke Fitz Warine's champion), and many motifs of the Anglo-Norman tale reappear in the later Robin Hood ballads—outlaw life in the greenwood, preying only upon particular enemies and not upon others, and prison rescues by trickery and by force. But this is the only Anglo-Norman prose romance that has survived.

3. Latin Prose Fiction in England

After the introduction of Christianity, Latin became the secondary language of most of the learned people in the British Isles. Although a majority of the Latin writings by British authors were religious, two works by Nennius and Geoffrey of Monmouth are fiction, masquerading as history. In classical times, Ennius, Virgil, and Livy had popularized the fiction that the Roman state had been founded by the Trojan Aeneas. Though Rome fell, its fictions persisted, and the new European states in imitation forged Trojan origins for themselves. As early as the middle of the seventh century, Fredegarius Scholasticus claimed that the Franks took their name from Francio, a descendant of Priam;[7] and in the ninth century, the Briton

Nennius reported that the island of Britain was first occupied by Brutus, grandson of Aeneas of Troy.[8]

Nennius was the first of the British romance historians. His *Historia Brittonum*, c. 830, was in part compiled from now-lost works whose authors had evidently exercised considerable creative imagination. Nennius did not give a connected account of the early events of British history, was uncritical in his handling of sources, and was more interested in marvels and exciting stories than factual accuracy. After a brief sketch of the six ages of the world and of the descendants of Dardanus who built Troy, he tells the story of Brutus, son of Ascanius and grandson of Aeneas, who accidentally kills his father while hunting; is exiled from Italy and wanders through the islands of the Tyrrhenian Sea; goes to Gaul, where he founds Tours; and finally comes to Britain, which has been inhabited by his descendants ever since (chap. 10).

Nennius also elaborated the story of Guorthigirn (Vortigern), who had welcomed the Saxons under Hencgist and had married his daughter. Guorthigirn begins to build a fortress in Guined (in Wales), but every night the building materials disappear. The boy Ambrosius explains that two dragons fight beneath the uncompleted walls of the fortress and that the red dragon (symbolizing the British) would drive out the white (the Saxons) (chaps. 31-48—Ambrosius becomes Merlin in Geoffrey of Monmouth). After Guorthigirn's death, Arthur, the "dux bellorum" (leader of armies, not king), was victorious against the Saxons in twelve battles, in the last of which, at Mount Badon, he slew nine hundred and sixty enemies with his own hand (chap. 56). So in Nennius, we have the earliest known references to the colonization of Britain by the Trojan Brutus, to the story of Vortigern's tower and the two dragons, and to the British leader Arthur.

Nennius wrote during the rule of Saxon kings. Three centuries later, under the Normans, Geoffrey of Monmouth in his *Historia regum Britanniae* (c. 1136) produced one of the greatest romance histories of all time, a fitting rival to the earlier books of Livy's *History of Rome*, from which he manufactured his own account of Belinus and Brennius.[9] Geoffrey, who was born in Wales, the last homeland of the ancient Britons, had noticed that, except for fragmentary details in Gildas and Bede (he did not mention Nennius, who was his most important source), he could find no connected account of the British (that is, Celtic) kings of England; so he proceeded to fabricate one. He created, almost entirely by himself, the whole legendary history of the British people, from the coming of Brutus shortly after the Trojan war until the death of the last British king, Cadualadrus, at Rome in 689 A.D.

Geoffrey pretended that he was merely the translator into Latin of a British, or Breton, book that had been given to him by his friend Walter, Archdeacon of Oxford; but no such British book is known to exist, and most of Geoffrey's work is patently fictitious. What he did was to invent or adapt a series of one hundred and six names, many of them eponyms (often place names), which provided continuously linked reigns of British kings for some nineteen hundred years. He was the inventor of, among others, the stories of Locrine, Bladud (who was killed trying to fly), King Lear and his three daughters, Gorboduc, Cymbeline and his sons Guiderius and Arviragus, Merlin's transportation of Stonehenge from Ireland, and the victorious reign of King Arthur (who dies in 542).

Geoffrey created, all at once, most of the mythical history of Celtic Britain. His work was immediately popular, and it spread, with remarkable speed for an age of manuscript transmission, all over Europe. Nearly two hundred manuscripts survive—more than those of a true history, such as Bede's. Geoffrey's popularity resulted principally from his art as a narrator. He chose interesting stories and told them well. Though he dealt with the reigns of a hundred and six kings, he devoted the greater part of his space to three: Brutus, Belinus, and Arthur. In dealing with individual stories, he knew how to select and focus details and events and how to structure his episodes to make them interesting. For example, his account of Arthur's campaign in Gaul, instead of being cluttered with irrelevant episodes, is centered on his fight with Frollo, the French governor. Geoffrey was also skillful in enhancing interest through peripeteia—Arthur is no sooner crowned than he is attacked by the Saxons; at the Whitsuntide feast to celebrate his conquests, when all is apparently peaceful, envoys arrive from Rome demanding tribute; he sets out to invade Rome, but on the way receives news of the rebellion of his nephew Modred; he kills Modred and then is himself mortally wounded.

Nennius was not printed until 1691, so the stories he told were known mainly through their adaptation by Geoffrey. Geoffrey's *Historia* circulated widely in manuscript and was printed at Paris in 1508 and 1517, but only a few later historians and antiquaries were directly acquainted with his Latin texts. However, the materials Geoffrey embellished and invented were soon made part of the chronicle histories of England, through which they reached a wider audience. Among the best known of these were Higden's *Polychronicon*, printed by Caxton in Trevisa's translation in 1482; the *Brut* or *Chronicles of England*, a fourteenth-century English translation of a French prose redaction of Wace's versification of Geoffrey, extant in more than a hundred and twenty manuscripts and printed by Caxton and others in thirteen editions between 1480 and 1528; Fabyan's *New Chronicles of England* (1516); Polydore Vergil's *Anglica historia* (1534); and Lanquet and Cooper's *Chronicle* (1549), which by itself or excerpted in Grafton's *Abridgement* and Stow's *Summary* had twenty-four editions by 1618. In addition, Holinshed (in his *Chronicles*) and Stow (in his *Annals*) translated literally long passages of Geoffrey in their accounts of early British history.

People read Geoffrey, either first or second hand, primarily for his narratives; only the more credulous accepted him as an historian. Within half a century, his compatriot Giraldus Cambrensis refuted his fiction with another fiction, for he told of a Welsh prophet who was plagued by evil spirits: if a book of the Gospels was laid in his lap, the spirits would vanish; but if a copy of Geoffrey's *Historia* was substituted, the spirits would cluster about him in greater numbers than before.[10] Most of the historians were skeptical or cautious, but still included Geoffrey's stories so that their histories would be more interesting. John Rastell was among the most skeptical of the historians, for he branded Geoffrey's history "a feigned story," and yet he too epitomized his earlier account of the British kings because it contained "examples of princes that wisely and virtuously governed" and showed how tyranny and vice "were ever by the stroke of God punished" (*The Pastime of People*, 1530, A2). Holinshed did not doubt the existence of Arthur, but he was skeptical of his European conquests, because, "as there is not any approved author who doth speak of any such doings, the Britains are thought to have registered mere fables instead of true matters, upon a vain desire to advance...their...champion, as the Frenchmen have done their Roland" (*Chronicles*, 1587,5:xii). Though Holinshed doubted the historical accuracy of some of Arthur's doings, he included without demur in his own history Geoffrey's equally fabulous stories of Locrine, Lear, Gorboduc, Cymbeline, and others, and so provided plots for

Shakespeare and his fellow dramatists. Though Geoffrey was neither a scholar nor a statesman, he created more history than the greatest historians who ever wrote or the greatest conquerors who ever reigned.

4. Old English and Middle English Prose Fiction

The Saxons and other fifth-century Germanic invaders from the Continent established their own language in Britain. They learned to write from Christian missionaries, producing 189 manuscripts in Old English that still exist. Many Old English religious treatises and a few poems survive but only one work of longer prose fiction is extant, *Apollonius of Tyre*, a literal translation done in the eleventh century of a fifth-century continental Latin work, now preserved in a single manuscript defective in its central portion.[11] It is a Greek-romance type story of fantastic adventure and farfetched coincidence, economically related in chronological order in the third person. The emphasis falls on the narrative, in which three stories are interlaced with some conversation, a few set speeches, a letter, and a minimum of description. The characters are one-dimensional types, the style plain, the pace swift, and the plot preposterous. The main interest of the anonymous author is in describing unusual and emotionally charged situations—incest, surprising coincidences, a girl who preserves her virginity in a brothel, the reunion of a father with his lost child and of a husband with his supposedly dead wife. It is full of the irrational but exciting fantasies of romance, which appealed to the Old-English translator and continued to appeal to a variety of readers for centuries. More than a hundred manuscripts exist of the Latin text, which was translated into most European languages, versified by an anonymous Middle-English poet, and again versified by Gower in his *Confessio Amantis*. It was translated into English prose from French prose by Robert Copland in 1510, and again by Laurence Twyne in 1576; Twyne's prose, with Gower's verse, was the source of the play of *Pericles* attributed to Shakespeare; and this play, in turn, was the basis of another prose version by George Wilkins in 1608 and of a play by George Lillo in 1738. In our century, T.S. Eliot meditated upon the story in his *Marina* (1930). Well known throughout the Middle Ages, its fictional technique influenced considerably the structure of the later French romances and their literary descendants.

The translation of *Apollonius of Tyre* is the only work of longer prose fiction that survives from Old English times. In Middle English, a blank period of more than three hundred years follows until the beginning of the fifteenth century when longer prose fiction seems not to have been produced, or at least has not survived. Actually, during these centuries the art of fictional narrative flourished in England as it never had before, but the medium was verse rather than prose. From these three centuries we have almost ninety metrical romances (among the best of which are *Sir Orfeo* and *Sir Gawain and the Green Knight*), the moral tales of Gower, and the verse narratives of Chaucer, which brought the art of story telling to the highest level it had achieved in England. In France, the shift from verse to prose had taken place in the thirteenth century with the massive compilation of the so-called "Vulgate" version of the Arthurian romances. But in England, we have to wait until the fifteenth century for long fictional narratives in prose, and even then only ten translations or adaptations from Latin and French are extant before the introduction of printing by Caxton in 1476. Five of these are religious; another is a classical pseudo-biography; and four others are romances, including Sir Thomas Malory's collection of Arthurian narratives completed by 1470.

The earliest of the religious narratives is *The Three Kings of Cologne* (c. 1400), which tells the biblical story of the visit of the Magi to the infant Jesus, continues with their return to their own countries, and supplements the narrative with lengthy accounts of the marvels of the East. Two others are translations of French verse allegories composed early in the fourteenth century by Guillaume de Deguileville: *The Pilgrimage of the Soul* (1413, printed by Caxton in 1483) and *The Pilgrimage of the Life of the Manhood* (c. 1430), first-person dream visions recounted for purposes of religious instruction which contain much doctrine and little narrative. A fourth is *The Life and Martyrdom of Saint Katherine* (of Alexandria) extant in a single manuscript (c. 1430), a wholly fictitious life adding a later account of her lineage and conversion to an earlier account of her martyrdom. During the Middle Ages saints' lives were the favorite reading of the literate population, both lay and religious alike, because they combined serious religious instruction with sensational martyrdoms and miracles. Most of these were originally written in Latin, but were later translated or adapted into English.[12] Charlotte D'Evelyn lists almost three hundred saints' lives written in Middle English, but most of these are in verse.[13] Those in prose are short epitomes—only the life of St. Katherine survives in versions of more than short-story length. The fifth religious narrative is a translation, made about 1450, of the widely popular twelfth-century Latin *Barlam and Josaphat*—a biography, based on the life of Buddha, portraying the ideals of Christian asceticism.

The classical pseudo-biography is the anonymous *Life of the Great Alexander*, translated about 1430 from the tenth-century *Historia de Preliis*. This is a complete life of the conqueror in which a few historical details are overlaid with much apocryphal material. The author is more interested in the marvels of nature and the religions of the East than in events, so he has more description and discussion than narration. The earliest of the four romances, *King Ponthus and the Fair Sidone*, is a translation made about 1450 of a late fourteenth-century French prose adapation of the twelfth-century Anglo-Norman poem *Horn et Rimenild*, which is partly transformed into an educational tract. The second romance is a translation made about 1450 of the thirteenth-century French Vulgate prose *L'estoire de Merlin*, which greatly elaborates on the brief mentions of Merlin by Geoffrey of Monmouth, reduces the fighting and increases the lovemaking by providing him with a mistress, Nimiane, and also recounts the life of King Arthur until the conclusion of his successful war on Rome and the birth of Lancelot. It is a third-person narrative supposedly based upon a book written by the hermit Blase. After each important series of events, the author has Merlin visit Blase and give him a report of what has happened, so that "by his book have we the knowing thereof"; but the fiction of the "book" is not consistently maintained, for the author does not attempt to have Merlin present at all the events that are reported. The third romance is a prose epitome made about 1460 of Hue de Rotelande's Anglo-Norman poem *Ipomedon*, composed about 1190. The story is told in the third person by an omniscient author who follows his "book"; he reports action, conversation, and soliloquies, and he also invades the minds of his characters to discover motivation. The plot has the merit of being focused on a single hero and heroine, though it is artificial in the extreme. The action is sustained only by Ipomedon's pretence to prefer hunting to knightly deeds, his pretence to be a fool, and his pretence to be overcome by the giant Leonyn. Why readers should have been interested in following such an arbitrarily manipulated series of events is difficult to understand; nevertheless, the Anglo-Norman poem apparently enjoyed some popularity, for two earlier Middle-English verse translations of about 1350 and 1400 survive, one of which was printed by Wynkyn de Worde about 1528. The fourth romance is the best known, *The Whole Book of King Arthur and of His Noble Knights of the Round Table*, which the knight prisoner Sir Thomas Malory completed by 1470, and which William Caxton printed in a slightly edited and abbreviated form as *Le Morte D'Arthur* in 1485.

Arthurian stories became extraordinarily popular after Geoffrey of Monmouth. Within less than twenty years, Geoffrey's Latin prose was translated into Anglo-Norman verse in Wace's *Roman de Brut* (1155), which added the round table; fifty years later, Wace was adapted into English verse in Layamon's *Brut* (c.1205); and later still, in the late fourteenth or early fifteenth century, came the alliterative *Morte Arthure*. But after Geoffrey, the second great creator of Arthurian legend was the French court poet Chrétien de Troyes, who between 1170 and 1190 composed five long poems partly set at the court of King Arthur. In his *Perceval*, or *Le conte de graal*, he provided the beginning of the Grail Legend; and in his *Lancelot* or *Le chevalier de la charrette*, he invented the story of Lancelot's adulterous love affair with Guinevere. While Geoffrey had created for the English a hero, Arthur—a mighty soldier and conqueror of almost all Europe—Chrétien reduced him to inconsequence and made him a cuckold. In England, the French story of Lancelot and Guinevere's adultery was retold only by the anonymous author of the stanzaic *Morte Arthure* (c. 1400) and by Malory; the other English accounts followed Geoffrey in presenting Arthur without Lancelot.

In the early thirteenth century, between 1215 and 1230, the Arthurian stories of Wace, Chrétien, and others were redacted into French prose by a number of different authors working independently, and these prose versions were collected together in an enormous cycle of some million and a half words, which has been designated the "Vulgate Arthurian Cycle." This is the earliest and longest example of continental European vernacular prose fiction. It became extraordinarily popular and was preserved in whole or in part in more than a hundred manuscripts, many of which differ considerably from one another in content, organization, and details of phrasing.

Instead of the straightforward linear story told by Geoffrey, the French prose Vulgate Cycle is immensely complicated and interwoven. A narrative thread is started, then dropped, and another thread is taken up, and another, and another, until finally a return is made to the first thread, which is again dropped and interwoven with other stories. This is the technique of *entrelacement*, earlier found in the *Odyssey*, in Ovid's *Metamorphoses*, in the Greek romances, and later in Boiardo and Ariosto, Sidney and Spenser. The Vulgate Cycle is composed of five related narratives: *L'estoire del Saint Graal*, *L'estoire de Merlin*, *Li livres de Lancelot*, *La queste del Saint Graal*, and *La mort le roi Artu*.

Malory's *Book of King Arthur*, which is the longest and most complete collection of Arthurian stories in English, includes all the narratives gathered together in the French prose Vulgate Cycle (except *L'estoire del Saint Graal*, which deals with events before the begetting of Arthur) and adds the romances of Gareth and of Tristram, the latter of which takes up more than a third of Malory's "Book." In his manuscript, Malory divided his work into eight sections. According to Eugène Vinaver,[14] their subjects and sources are the following:

(1) The Tale of King Arthur, from the French prose *Suite de Merlin* (a text slightly different from and later than the Vulgate *Estoire de Merlin*); (2) Arthur and Lucius, from the English alliterative poem *Morte Arthure*; (3) Launcelot, three selections from the Vulgate *Livres de Lancelot* plus material from unidentified sources; (4) Gareth (for which no source has been found); (5) Tristram, from the French prose *Tristan* of about 1230; (6) The Quest of the Grail, from the Vulgate *Queste del Saint Graal*;(7) Launcelot and Guinevere, from the Vulgate *Mort Artu*, the English stanzaic *Morte Arthur*, a prose version of Chrétien's *Charrette*, and an unidentified source for the third episode of the Tournament and the fifth episode of Sir Urry; and (8) The Death of Arthur, mainly from the English stanzaic *Morte Arthur.*

Malory followed his sources quite closely and did not often invent episodes. In the Arthur and Lucius section, for example, which is based on the English alliterative *Morte Arthure*, whole passages of alliterative verse are written without change as prose. But he epitomized his sources and reduced them to between one-half and one-eighth of their original length. He also simplified the narrative by disentangling the interwoven threads and making each thread a single, unified story. His style at first was formless and monotonous, a jumble of simple declarative phrases connected by "and"; as he continued, however, he improved, and his naive simplicity had greater appeal than the ostentatious tricks of more sophisticated authors. His last section, on the death of Arthur, is justly admired as the finest achievement of medieval prose romance in England. His accomplishment here is partly because of the excellence of the particular English verse original he was following, but also is the result of his increased skill as an adapter and his increased competence as a writer of simple, effective prose.

The critical questions more recently debated have concerned the unity of Malory's work and the extent of his originality. To see Malory's own qualities as a narrator and creator of fiction, readers should look at those parts of his book where he appears to be working most independently—the best example of which is the Tale of Launcelot. The first half of this part is based on the French prose Vulgate *Lancelot*; for the last half, no specific, immediate source has been found. In the first half, Malory does not follow his source consecutively, but translates a short series of episodes from the early part of the French tale, skips a hundred pages and translates a short section from the middle, then skips another hundred pages and translates three more episodes from the end; after that, he goes on independently or shifts to an unidentified source. Malory's Tale of Launcelot is episodic in structure, a series of independent incidents whose only relationship to one another is that in each of them the protagonist is Launcelot. A theme is stated at the beginning—"in all tournaments he passed all other knights"—and repeated at the end—"so at that time Sir Launcelot had the greatest name of any knight of the world." He is also shown to be impervious to all feminine blandishments, except Guinevere's.

Chance, not causation, links one episode to another; the various characters meet by accident after wandering over a featureless landscape, and it makes no difference whether one episode precedes or follows another. There are giants and enchantments and even some humor—Launcelot finds a bed in a pavilion in a forest and goes to sleep in it, but at night he awakes feeling a "rough beard kissing him": the knight Belleus, who has made an assignation with his mistress for that night, in the dark has crept into the bed thinking Launcelot is she. So we have a string of disconnected episodes, varying in tone. But Malory does not keep track of even this simple structure very well. At one point, Launcelot exchanges armor with Kay, and in the two following episodes he defeats groups of knights who fight with him because they think he is the easy-to-overcome Kay; in the three following episodes, he is in his own armor; in the final episode, when he returns to court, he is back in Kay's armor again and makes quite a point of revealing his disguise. The place where Launcelot resumed his own armor is the place where Malory stopped translating the Vulgate Lancelot; clearly, he switched to another source and did not keep track of his story well enough to maintain Launcelot in Kay's armor rather than his own.

5. Prose Fiction from England's First Printing Press

During the first thousand years of "English literary history," from the coming of the Angles and Saxons in the fifth century until the introduction of printing in the fifteenth, only eleven longer works of prose fiction in the vernacular have survived. None of these was an entirely original composition since all were translations or adaptations of works written originally in Latin or French; until nearly the end of the fifteenth century, almost all fictional narrative was in verse.

When William Caxton set up his printing press in Westminster in 1476 the new machine made possible the distribution of books more cheaply and in greater numbers than ever before. Gradually, people interested in fiction turned from listening to reading; just as gradually, the vehicle for narratives changed from verse to prose. From the Norman Conquest to the death of Chaucer, all surviving English fictional narratives are in verse; since the eighteenth century, most fictional narratives have been in prose. If our own age is a time of prose, the Middle Ages were a period of verse. The Renaissance was in between—an age of both verse and prose.

Printing from movable type was invented in Germany by Johan Gutenberg before 1450, and within twenty-five years the new invention had spread into all countries of Europe except Scandinavia and Russia. By 1500, the half century called the "incunabulum" or swaddling clothes stage of printing, some forty thousand editions had been produced in more than a hundred different cities. The invention of printing made possible the production of more copies of books in half a century than had been copied by hand in the preceding thousand years. In England, the earliest age of the printed book is charted by the Pollard and Redgrave Short Title Catalogue (1926), which lists all surviving editions of books printed in Britain or for the British market from the beginning of printing until 1640; the revised edition of the STC (2 vols. 1976–86) lists more than thirty thousand editions produced in those 165 years. Currently almost forty thousand editions of English books are being published every year. England was somewhat backward in adopting the new art of printing. Caxton himself was a publisher rather than a printer, since his journeymen set the type and worked the presses. He was a businessman who had spent thirty years in the Burgundian states on the Continent as a merchant and diplomatic agent. He learned the art of printing in Cologne, first set up his own press in Bruges, and then returned to England. In some seventeen years, until his death in 1491, he issued over a hundred editions of about seventy different titles. In order to provide copy for his press, he himself translated, mainly from French, a considerable number of the books he published. Of his forty English prose titles, twenty-nine were his own translations, and more than a third of these were longer works of prose fiction.

His first book, printed at Bruges about 1475, was *The Recuyell of the Histories of the Troy*, his own translation of a French work that had been composed by Raoul Le Fèvre only ten years earlier. About 1477, a year after setting up his press in England, he published *The History of Jason*, again his own translation of another work by Le Fèvre. In April 1480 he completed his translation of what he called Ovid's "Methamorphose," not from Ovid's Latin but from a French prose version of the fourteenth-century *Ovidius Moralisatus*. This work was apparently never printed. In 1481, he departed from classical subjects and published the medieval beast fable *Reynard the Fox*, his own translation of a Dutch version that had been printed in 1479. In 1483, as part of his translation from the French of *The Fables of Aesop*, he published *The Life of Aesop*. In 1485, he published another pseudo-biography, *Charles the Great King of France*, his own translation of the French prose *Fier a bras*, a Charlemagne romance that had been printed in 1483. In the same year, he published *Paris and Vienne*, another romance translated from French. In 1489, he published his translations of two French romances, *Blanchardine and Eglantine* and *The Four Sons of Aymon*, the latter also dealing with events at the court of Charlemagne. Finally in 1490, the year before his death, he returned to the classical subjects with which he had begun and published *Eneydos*—not Virgil's poem but his own translation of a French prose redaction only remotely related to Virgil's original. In addition to his own translations of ten romances, pseudo-histories, and biographies, he also printed, in 1483, the anonymous English translation (made in 1413) of Deguileville's *The Pilgrimage of the Soul*, and in 1485 Malory's *Le Morte D'Arthur*. Caxton was an awkwardly literal translator with little sense of style, but through his translations, in the short space of seventeen years, he gave his countrymen more prose fiction, albeit translations not original works, than was extant from the preceding thousand years.

6. From Caxton to Queen Elizabeth

Between the death of Caxton in 1491 and the accession of Queen Elizabeth in 1558, the production of English translations of prose fiction continued at an accelerating pace. Compared to the ten translations of prose fiction before Caxton, and the ten by Caxton himself, twenty-two were produced in the following sixty-five years. Chivalric romances, of which a total of nine survive, continued to be the most popular fictional kind. Three were anonymous translations: *The Three Kings' Sons*, an account of the rivalry of the sons of the kings of France, Scotland, and England for the hand of Iolante, who is won by Philip of France; *Melusine*, the tale of a fairy who is a beautiful woman six days of the week but turns into a serpent on Saturdays, the legendary ancestress of the house of Lusignan; and *King William of Palermo*, the story of Alphouns the friendly werewolf.

Three other romances were translated by Henry Watson (who worked for Caxton's successor, the printer Wynkyn de Worde), all made from recently printed French editions: *King Ponthus*, a new translation; *Valentine and Orson*, the story of two brothers, one of whom is brought up by a bear; and *Oliver of Castile*, about Oliver and his friend Arthur, his courtship of the daughter of the king of England, and the assistance given him by the ghost of the White Knight—a story upon which Peele drew for his *Old Wives' Tale*. Robert Copland, who also worked for de Worde, translated *Helyas, Knight of the Swan*, the supposed ancestor of the historical Godfrey of Bouillon, whose brothers are turned into swans through the machinations of an evil grandmother, but are eventually restored to human shape (in spite of apparent similarities, no relationship exists between this story and that of Lohengrin).

Lastly, John Bourchier, Lord Berners, improved his French and whiled away the time when he was governor of Calais by translating two very long romances. The first was *Arthur of Little Britain* (not the English King Arthur, but a prince of Brittany), in which Arthur, with the help of the Fairy Queen Proserpine and the necromancer Steven, after many adventures wins Florence, daughter of the king of Sorolois. The second was *Huon of Bordeaux*, a complicated offshoot of the Charlemagne cycle, in which Huon, with the help of the dwarf Oberon, king of the fairies, accomplishes a seemingly impossible task set him by Charlemagne and wins Esclarmonde, daughter of the admiral of Babylon, and survives the treachery of his brother, Gerard. This has four continuations narrating further marvelous adventures of Huon, the marriage of his daughter Claryet, the trials of her daughter Ide (who experiences a change of sex and becomes a man), and the travels of Ide's son, Croysant, who eventually becomes emperor of Rome. From this romance, Shakespeare derived the character of the fairy king Oberon in his *A Midsummer Night's Dream*.

In addition to these nine romances, there were translations of seven classical stories, or medieval stories with classical backgrounds. Robert Copland made a second translation, this time from French, of Apollonius of Tyre; Thomas Paynell translated, also from French, Dares Phrygius' Latin *The Destruction of Troy*, which pretended to be the account of a Trojan eyewitness; William Baxter translated, from Greek, *The Books of Xenophon Containing... the Education of Cyrus*, a fictionalized biography of the founder of the Persian empire portraying the ideal ruler; Lord Berners translated, from French, Diego de San Pedro's Spanish *Cárcel del amor*, which is set in Macedonia; and John Clerc translated, also via French, San Pedro's *Arnalte y Lucenda*, a love story set in Thebes during the reign of Cadmus. Also printed were anonymous translations of the Latin *Seven Wise Masters of Rome*, a frame tale containing fifteen stories about the evil deeds done by children to parents and by women to men, and of the Dutch *The Life of Virgilius*, a collection of anecdotes about a magician (not the poet) in the time of Remus.

Three miscellaneous translations appear to mirror contemporary situations: from Latin, *Eurialus and Lucrece*, the love story which had been written by Pius II before he became pope; and from German, the jest-book biographies of *Howleglas* (Til Eulenspiegel) and the *Parson of Kalenborow* (Kalenberg). And finally, there were three translations of religious narratives: *Robert the Devil*, from French, the story of a grievous sinner who achieved salvation by penance; *The Destruction of Jerusalem by Vespasian and Titus*, also from French, an entirely legendary treatment of the historical event; and William Baldwin's translation, from Latin, *Wonderful News of the Death of Paul the Third*, a first-person account in epistolary form of an imaginary descent to hell satirizing the late pope.

7. Overview, 1050–1558

Subjects

From Old-English times to the accession of Queen Elizabeth, only forty-three translations of longer works of fiction into English prose are extant: twenty-eight of these are from French, eight from Latin, two from Dutch, two from German, one from Greek, and none directly from either Italian or Spanish. Two titles were translated twice: the Latin *Apollonius of Tyre* and the French *Ponthus and the Fair Sidone*. The largest proportion of the total, eighteen in all (including one duplicate), consists of chivalric romances. Lord Berners' *Huon of Bordeaux* was the last sixteenth-century English translation of a medieval romance. Romances continued to be popular, but after the mid-sixteenth century they were translated from Renaissance Spanish versions, such as Margaret Tyler's translation of Ortuñes de Calahorra's *Mirror of Princely Deeds* (c. 1578), or Anthony Mundy's later translations of the Palmerin and Amadis cycles, or from the highly stylized seventeenth-century French romances by Honore D'Urfé, la Calprenête, and the Scudèrys.

Sixteen narratives (including one duplicate) were written on classical subjects or with classical backgrounds; only seven on religious subjects; and four which give the appearance of mirroring contemporary or nearly contemporary situations: the beast fable *Reynard the Fox* (though it stems from a Latin poem of the eleventh century), the jest biographies of *Howleglas* and the *Parson of Kalenborow*, and Pius II's love story *Eurialus and Lucrece*. The interest in classical subjects is noteworthy. English readers were apparently more attracted to the court of King Priam of Troy than to the court of King Arthur of Britain, for only the prose *Merlin* (which remained in manuscript) and Caxton's publication of Malory were devoted to Arthur, while thirteen other narratives were set in classical Greece or Rome. Almost all the stories were about distant lands and ancient times. Only the anonymous *Merlin*, Malory's *Book of King Arthur*, Borde's *Scoggin's Jests*, Baldwin's *Beware the Cat*, and the pseudonymous *Image of Idleness* have their settings in England, and only the last three deal with the England of the authors' own time. The earliest longer works of fiction all dealt with the antique and the exotic.

Narrative techniques

The most complex narrative form, the interlace, is found in the very earliest translated work of English fiction, the West Saxon version of *Apollonius of Tyre*. It appears frequently in the period under discussion and continues in use afterwards, in the revised version of Sidney's *Arcadia* in 1584 and beyond in long seventeenth-century romances such as Roger Boyle, Earl of Orrery's *Parthenissa*, which was printed in six volumes between 1654 and 1669. *Valentine and Orson*, translated from a late fifteenth-century French original by Henry Watson in 1502, is the most complicated early example. Six main characters or groups of characters appear, plus a large number of minor figures, whose interrelated actions are narrated in more than forty interlaced episodes.

But most of the forty-three translated narratives consist of simple linear plots presented in chronological order—usually a whole life, like *The Life of the Great Alexander*, which begins with his being fathered by the magician Anectanabus, tells of his youth, his conquests, his travels and the marvels he sees, his romance with Roxana, and his death by the treachery of a false friend. This simple chronological story line is found even in the bulky *Huon of Bordeaux*, whose action extends through four generations—from the youth of Huon to the death of his grandson, Croysant.

The best of this linear type is *Paris and Vienne*, written in French prose in 1432 and translated and printed by Caxton in 1485. It is a Romeo and Juliet type story of parental opposition to young love with a happy marriage ending. The focus is on the two lovers only, with no deviation into irrelevancies. Only one story is told, and it is not interlaced with others. The setting is high society, but the events are familiar, there are no miraculous happenings, and all the action is credible. Though most of the story is straight narrative, a fair amount of conversation appears, and some use is made of letters. The characters are little individualized, but boldly sketched. The lady Vienne is the dominant figure who makes the decisions and suffers; Paris is the docile lover who nevertheless performs great deeds of arms. They are nearly perfect patterns of faithful lovers who act and speak always with the most exact propriety and the noblest of sentiments.

Point of View

All but five of these forty-three translations are told in the third person by an uncharacterized narrator. Only rarely does the author comment on the action, as when the author of *Charles the Great King of France* interjects, "O wicked Ganellon," or when Malory comments, "So fareth the love nowadays, soon hot soon cold; this is no stability, but the old love was not so" (18.25). The characters are sketched almost entirely from without; seldom does the author give any hint of their feelings or of the workings of their minds. However, the French Deguileville presents both of his personification allegories as dreams in which he observes himself; the pseudonymous Esquillus writes his *Wonderful News of the Death of Paul the Third* as a personal letter; and the Spanish Diego de San Pedro offers both his novels in the first person, in which he as author is an observer of the action, but not a principal participant in it.

San Pedro's *Cárcel del amor,* written in 1492 and translated into English some thirty years later, is technically the most accomplished work of prose fiction produced in the fifteenth century, partly because of the skillful maintenance of the first-person point of view. The novel is divided into sections headed "Author," "Leriano," "Laureola," etc., in which the author in his own person narrates and comments, and also reports the speeches spoken and letters written by the other characters. But his earlier *Arnalte y Lucenda* (1491, translated into English in 1542) is even more interesting because of the way in which the principal character is unwittingly made to reveal himself. The first-person narrator, while trying to invoke sympathy for the wrongs supposedly done to him, reveals his egotism and his selfish inability to comprehend the feelings of others. Though San Pedro has been disparaged as a sentimental novelist, he was certainly not unaware of the ironic overtones of his first-person narration.

The Comic

The producers of early English prose fiction were a serious lot, apparently more interested in fighting and lovemaking than in jesting. Few humorous episodes appear in all of Old-English literature. In Malory, occasional situations raise a smile, as when the knight Belleus gets into Launcelot's bed thinking he is his mistress or when King Mark flees in terror from Sir Dagonet, King Arthur's fool, under the impression that he is Launcelot. Caxton's translation of *Reynard the Fox* contains some humor, though the laughter of this story is the laughter of cruelty rather than of good spirits. In one episode, the fox creeps through a hole into the house of a priest and steals his fowls; the priest sets a trap in the hole; the fox tells the cat that he will find many mice if he goes into the hole; the cat does so, is caught in the trap, and soundly beaten. This sadistic kind of humor apparently had its attractions, for the author of *Gammer Gurton's Needle* adapted the incident in the scene where Diccon persuades Doctor Rat to creep through a hole into Dame Chat's house, where he is caught and beaten. And even Cervantes thought the spectacle of Don Quixote having his teeth knocked out was laughable.

Two of the fifteen stories of *The Seven Wise Masters of Rome,* a translation (c. 1493) of an early fourteenth-century Latin text, have a comic turn. The fourth story is about a husband who locks his wandering wife out of their house at night, but she tricks him into opening the door and then locks him out in turn. This had been told in the twelfth century by Petrus Alphonsus and was later used by Deloney in his *Jack of Newbury.* The fourteenth story is a version of the tale told in Petronius' *Satyricon* of the Ephesian matron, a tale which exemplifies the fickleness of women. *Howleglas* is a jester, though not all of his tricks are funny, and too many of his jokes are of the scatological kind, such as the one Baldwin later used in the episode of Streamer's "presciental pills." Only four of the twenty-two episodes in *The Life of Virgilius* are humorous. The general favorite, often repeated, is the anecdote of Virgil in the basket, which Deloney adapted to the discomfiture of Cutbert by Bosom in *Thomas of Reading.* The third of the early jest-book biographies, *The Parson of Kalenborow,* has some humor, if it can be called that, again of a mainly scatological variety. Andrew Borde continued the tradition of the jest-book biography in *Scoggin's Jests,* which contains a number of highly amusing stories. Though humor arrived late and at first made only a fitful appearance in English prose fiction, it was firmly established by the mid-sixteenth century. Significantly, the two earliest original works of longer English fiction, Baldwin's *Beware the Cat* and the pseudonymous *Image of Idleness,* are both comic novels of a high order of excellence.

NOTES

1. Kenneth H. Jackson, *The Oldest Irish Tradition* (Cambridge, 1964), 45.

2. Myles Dillon, *Celts and Aryans* (Simla, 1975) 70.

3. A translation of the first version was made by Winifred Faraday, *The Cattle Raid of Cou-alnge* (London, 1904); of the second by Joseph Dunn, *The Ancient Epic Tale of Táin Bó Cúalnge* (London, 1914), and more recently by Cecile O'Rahilly (Dublin, 1967). The most attractive and influential rendering of a reconstructed version of the entire cycle is Lady Augusta Gregory's *Cuchulain of Muirthemne* (London, 1902), which was used by Yeats, Synge, and other poets and playwrights of the Irish Revival. Myles Dillon, *Early Irish Literature* (Chicago, 1948), has an excellent account of the saga cycles.

4. Ed. Carl Selmer, *Navigatio Sancti Brendani Abbatis, from Early Latin Manuscripts,* University of Notre Dame Publications in Medieval Studies, 16 (1959); English tr. J.F. Webb, *Lives of the Saints* (1965). Epitomized in English verse in the *South English Legendary,* early fourteenth century, and in prose in Caxton's *Golden Legend,* 1483, separately printed by de Worde c. 1520. For later voyages in search of St. Brendan's island, see T.J. Westropp, *Proceedings of the Royal Irish Academy,* 30 (1912): 223–260.

5. Translated by Gwyn Jones and Thomas Jones (London, 1949).

6. The only extant manuscript was edited and translated for the Warton Club by Thomas Wright (London, 1855); a later translation was made by Alice Kemp-Welsh (London, 1904).

7. *Chronicarum Libri IV,* 2,5 (ed. Bruno Krusch, *Monumenta Germaniae Historica: Scriptores Rerum Merovingiarum,* 2 [1888]: 46).

8. *Historia Brittonum,* 2.10 (ed. Theodor Mommsen, *Monumenta Germaniae Historica: Auctorum Antiquissimorum Tomus xiii,* (1898), 150). There are English translations by J.A. Giles in *Six Old English Chronicles* (London, 1848), and by A.W. Wade-Evans (London, 1938).

9. Translated by Lewis Thorpe, *The History of the Kings of Britain* (London, 1966).

10. *Itinerarium Kambriae,* 1.5 (*Opera,* ed. J.S. Brewer and J.F. Dimock, 6 [1868]: 57—Rolls Series).

11. Summaries of the action of each of the English works discussed is given in Appendix 2, along with bibliographical information about early printings and scholarly editions. Omitted are the Old English prose translations from Latin, *Wonders of the East* and *Letter of Alexander to Aristotle,* because they are only of short-story length and, like the later *Travels of Sir John Mandeville,* are more descriptive than narrative.

12. "Legends of Individual Saints" in J. Burke Severs, ed., *A Manual of Writings in Middle English,* 2 (Hamden, Conn., 1970): 561–635.

13. In *A Manual of the Writings in Middle English 1050-1500,* ed. J. Burke Severs.

14. Eugène Vinaver, *The Works of Sir Thomas Malory,* 3 (Oxford, 1967): 1267-1663 passim.

Appendix 2
Plot Summaries of Longer
Fictional Prose Narratives in English to 1558

"Longer" here is arbitrarily defined as more than ten thousand words in length, "fictional" as an account of happenings that would not be accepted as factual by a modern historian, and "narrative" as a summary of the actions of a single character or group of characters. We therefore omit single short tales or collections of tales that belong to the history of the short story rather than to the novel.

Omitted as too short are the fifteenth-century *Siege of Troy* and *Siege of Thebes*, the Dublin Alexander Epitome, and the Porkington 10 MS *Siege of Jerusalem;* the sixteenth-century *Joseph of Arimathea, Frederick of Jennen, Mary of Nimeguen,* and Lord Morley's translation of Masuccio's 49th Novella; omitted as unconnected collections of short tales are *The Alphabet of Tales, Jacob's Well, The Book of the Knight of La Tour Landry* (two translations), the three English versions of the *Gesta Romanorum,* Caxton's *Aesop, A Hundred Merry Tales, Tales and Quick Answers, Dialogues of Creatures Moralized,* Borde's *Mad Men of Gotham, The Deceit of Women,* and *The Sack-full of News.* Also omitted are single short tales in longer non-narrative works, such as the story of Titus and Gesippus told in Elyot's *Governor* or short anecdotes about tricksters in *A Manifest Detection of Dice Play;* and shorter saints' lives, either in collections such as Caxton's *Golden Legend* or published individually, such as *The Life of Saint Winifred* and *The Life of Saint Brandon.*

We do, however, include collections of stories like *The Seven Wise Masters of Rome* and *Scoggin's Jests* that are unified either by a frame or by being parts of the biography of a single person. We omit, as being real history rather than fiction, Caxton's *Eracles* and also *Godfrey of Boulogne.* We also omit, as being primarily argumentative, descriptive, or expository rather than narrative, Chaucer's *Tale of Melibee, The Book of John Mandeville,* the translation of Buonaccorso da Montemagno's *Declamation of Nobles,* the dialogues of *Solomon and Marcolphus* and *The Demands Joyous,* Sir Thomas More's *Utopia* (in Latin, but translated into English in 1551), Christine de Pisan's *City of Ladies* and *Hundred Histories of Troy,* and Guevara's *Golden Book of Marcus Aurelius* (translated by Lord Berners and enlarged as *The Dial of Princes,* translated by Thomas North). Finally, we omit *Aurelio and Isabel* (1556), a translation from Italian into French, Spanish, and English of Juan de Flores' Spanish *Grisel y Mirabella,* because it is part of an elementary language manual—translated by a Netherlander for Netherlanders and printed in Antwerp—which forms no part of English literary history. Only two-thirds of the forty-seven items listed below appear in Arundel Esdaile's standard bibliography, *English Tales and Prose Romances to 1740* (1912).

Entries are listed alphabetically according to the first significant word in the title rather than by the last name of the author or translator: thus, *The faythfull and true storye of the destruction of Troye, compyled by Dares Phrygius* appears under DESTRUCTION OF TROY, not Dares Phrygius. Short titles of entries have been modernized, (thus, Aesop rather than Esope), while the full titles follow the spelling and punctuation of the first printed edition.

AENEID.
The boke [o]*f Eneydos,* W. Caxton, 1490; ed. M.T. Culley and F.J. Furnivall, EETSes 57, 1890. About 46,000 words. Translation by Caxton of the French prose *Livre des Eneydes,* Lyons, 1483.

This retains the main episodes of Virgil's narrative, but greatly changes it in details and in manner of presentation. Virgil's twelve-book epic structure, with its *in medias res* beginning and its flashbacks, is completely abandoned, and instead we have a chronological narrative in sixty-five chapters about chivalric "faits of arms." The story begins with the founding of Troy by Priam, pays extended attention to Dido, and ends with three chapters (whose substance is not found in Virgil at all) giving the later history of Aeneas and Lavinia and the Alban kings who succeeded them. Virgil's classical epic is transformed into a medieval romance.

AESOP.
"The lyf of Esope" in *The subtyl historyes and Fables of Esope,* translated by William Caxton in 1483 from Julian Macho's French translation (Lyon, 1480) of Heinrich Steinhöwel's Latin and German collection (Ulm, c. 1476). The "Fables" of Aesop (as well as the appended fables of Avianus, Alphonsus, and Poggio) are all short, but the "lyf" extends to about 17,000 words. It was printed by Caxton in 1484 and reached a twelfth edition by 1658, therefore becoming Caxton's second most popular translation. Ed. R.T. Lenaghan, Cambridge, Mass., 1967. The "lyf" stems from a Latin translation made in 1448 by Rinuccio da Castiglione of an eleventh-century Greek version. Caxton and his contemporaries probably considered it genuine biography, though no present-day scholar would accept any of its details as authentic. It is a collection of witty sayings and anecdotes of the kind found in jest books.

Aesop is born near Troy. He is hunchbacked, has an abnormally large head, cannot talk, but he is clever. A fellow slave steals figs and accuses Aesop of eating them. As Aesop cannot speak in his own defense, he makes himself vomit and only water comes up; but when the thief is made to vomit the figs appear. Later, Aesop is sold to a merchant and on the way to Ephesus decides to carry what is apparently the heaviest load, a pannier of bread; but the bread is eaten during the journey, so in the end he has the lightest load.
   The merchant sells him to the philosopher Exantus, to whom he gives wise answers to seemingly impossible questions. Exantus once wagered that he could drink all the water of the sea. When the day to make good his boast arrives, Aesop advises him to require his opponent first to keep the rivers from emptying their waters into the sea and so refilling it. Later, Aesop is made free by the Samians, and he secures remission of their tribute to Croesus by telling him fables. At Babylon, he adopts a son, named Enus, who wrongly accuses him of treason; when Aesop forgives him, he kills himself in remorse. Aesop explains to the king how a tower could be built without touching earth or heaven by tying small children to the feet of eagles who would lift them into the air to do the work. He then goes to Egypt, and afterwards to Greece, where the citizens of Delphi, angry at his telling them

they were of little worth, secrete a gold goblet in his baggage, accuse him of stealing it, and unjustly execute him. For this, the Delphians suffer pestilence and famine.

ALEXANDER.

The lyf of gret Alexander. An anonymous, slightly abridged translation, c. 1430, of the Archpresbyter Leo's Latin *Historia de Preliis,* c. 950. About 46,000 words. One MS. Ed. J.S. Westlake, EETS 143, 1913. A life of Alexander the Great, with lengthy digressions on the marvelous natural history, customs, and beliefs of India and the Indians.

The pseudo-biography opens with the begetting of Alexander upon Olympia by the magician Anectanabus, and next tells of Alexander's taming of the horse Bucephalus, his early conquest of Rome, and his founding of Alexandria. The central portion deals with his campaigns against Darius, who at first did not take him seriously and sent him a ball with the message that "it is more seemly that thou use child's games than deeds of arms." The text continues with Darius' defeat at the Granicus and his assassination by his own officers. Alexander buries him with honors, marries his daughter Roxana, and is crowned king of Persia. In the final portion, Alexander marches against Porus of India, whom he slays in single combat. There are long accounts of the marvels of India (the Amazons, the Basilisk that slays by its sight) and a lengthy correspondence between Alexander and Dindimus about the Brahmans. The Warden of the Holy Trees prophesies that Alexander will be poisoned by a friend. He continues his conquests, captures Babylon, receives a letter from Aristotle praising his virtues, is poisoned by Antipater, and dies at the age of thirty-two.

APOLLONIUS, KING OF TYRE.

Kynge Appolyn of Thyre. Translation by Robert Copland from the French *Apollin roy de Thire,* Geneva, c. 1482. About 23,000 words. Printed by Wynkyn de Worde, 1510, facsimile ed. E.W. Ashbee, London, 1870. For summary, see the Old English version below. Copland's translation has thirty-five chapters. He spells the proper names Anthiogus Appolyn, Archystrates, his daughter Archycastres, Tharcie, Tranquyle (for Stranguilio), his wife Dyonyse, and Prince Anthygoras.

APOLLONIUS OF TYRE.

Apollonius thaes tiriscan. Translation into West Saxon, c. 1050, of the Latin *Apollonius Tyrius,* composed in the sixth century. One MS defective in the middle; complete text probably 13,000 words. Ed. Benjamin Thorpe, 1834 (with English translation); another English translation by Michael Swanton, *Anglo-Saxon Prose,* 1975. A Latin romance fashioned after Greek models that provided the archetypal pattern for many of the medieval romances.

The tyrant of Antioch propounds a riddle which the young prince of Tyre, Apollonius, solves and in so doing reveals the tyrant's incest with his own daughter. Apollonius flees the tyrant's vengeance and is shipwrecked on the shore of Pentapolis, where a poor fisherman. shares with him his only garment. Apollonius says that if he does not repay the fisherman's kindness as soon as he is able, he would wish to be shipwrecked again. He gains the favor of the king, Arcestratus, whose daughter falls in love with him. He marries her, but does not reward the old fisherman. Later, he learns that the tyrant of Antioch has been killed by lightning from heaven and that he has gained the kingdom. He sets sail for Antioch, and during a storm his wife gives birth to a daughter and apparently dies herself. She is placed in a chest and cast into the sea; the chest floats to Ephesus, where she revives and becomes a priestess of Diana.

Meanwhile Apollonius, instead of continuing on to Antioch, sails to Tharsus where he leaves his newly-born daughter, Tharsia, in the care of Dionysias, wife of his friend Stranguilio; he then goes to Egypt, where he remains for fourteen years. When Tharsia is fourteen years old, her nurse reveals that she is not the daughter of Stranguilio but really the daughter of King Apollonius. Dionysias, jealous that the young men praise Tharsia above her own daughter, orders a slave to murder Tharsia; but before the slave can do so, the girl is carried off by pirates who sell her to a brothel keeper in Mitylene. Prince Athenagoras and other young men of Mitylene who visit the brothel are so affected by her tears that they refrain from attempting her virginity.

At this point, Apollonius returns to Tharsus for his daughter, is told that she is dead, and sails sadly to Tyre. A storm drives his ship to Mitylene, where he remains grieving in his cabin. Tharsia is sent to comfort him, and she tells the story of her life from which he recognizes her as his daughter. She then marries Prince Athenagoras. Apollonius dreams that he will not be able to return to Tyre unless he makes sacrifice to Diana; so he sails to Ephesus, where he tells the priestess the story of his life, and she reveals herself as his long-lost wife. He and his wife then visit her father at Pentapolis, who bequeaths them his kingdom and dies. At Pentapolis, Apollonius finally meets and rewards the old fisherman, after which Apollonius reigns peacefully for seventy-seven years.

ARNALTE AND LUCENDA.
A certayne treatye moste wyttely devysed orygynally wrytten in the spanyshe, lately Traducted in to Frenche entytled, l'amant mal traicte de s'amye. And nowe out of Frenche in to Englysshe, dedicat to the...lorde Henry (Howard) Erle of Surrey, R. Wyer, 1541[/2]. About 19,000 words. Translated by John Clerc from Nicholas de Herberay's 1539 French translation of Diego de San Pedro's Spanish *Arnalte y Lucenda*, 1491. A narrative consisting mainly of set speeches and letters.

The author tells how he comes to the house of a sorrowful knight, Arnalte, who promises to tell him his story if he will publish it so that ladies "may know the ill that a woman hath caused me to suffer." All that follows is the narration of Arnalte, although he occasionally reports speeches made in his absence so that the first-person point of view is not consistently maintained.

At the court of King Cadmus of Thebes, I fall in love with Lucenda [Arnalte explains to the author] and tell her she will cause my death if she does not return my affection, but she will not. I tell my friend Yerso, who lives next door to Lucenda, of my love. He invites me to his lodging, but I can catch no sight of Lucenda and pine away in melancholy. I tell my sister Belysa, who presents my suit to Lucenda [their speeches are given at length]. Finally Lucenda, for Belysa's sake, agrees to meet me. We meet in a church; I tell her that I have shown my constancy by my suffering and that she is obligated to relieve me. She allows me to kiss her hand. We part, my melancholy disappears, and I engage in normal recreations again. Later, I learn that Lucenda has married Yerso. I challenge Yerso and kill him in judicial combat. I then write to Lucenda, "Sithen I have taken him away from thee, I will give myself to thee." But when my sister delivers the letter, she finds that Lucenda has entered a nunnery. So I have retired to this solitary place, and you now know what I have suffered from love. [Here the first-person narrator, while trying to provoke sympathy for his case, reveals his egotistical selfishness and his inability to understand the feelings of others.]

ARTHUR.
The hoole book of kyng Arthur and of his noble knyghtes of the Rounde Table. Translation and adaptation by Sir Thomas Malory, completed by 1470, in eight sections, of the thirteenth-century French prose Merlin, Lancelot, Tristan, Graal, and Artu narratives, with the use of the fourteenth-century English alliterative *Morte Arthure*, the stanzaic *Morte Arthur*, and other sources. About 330,000 words. One manuscript, ed. Eugène Vinaver, 3 vols., Oxford, 1947, revised 1967. Edited and slightly abridged by William Caxton as *Le morte Darthur*, 1485, six editions by 1634, then none until 1816; thereafter many; Caxton's text modernized by Janet Cowen, 2 vols., 1969.

I. *The Tale of King Arthur* (Caxton i-iv). Uther Pendragon, disguised by the magician Merlin as the husband of Igrayne, begets a child upon her, who is named "Arthur" and is brought up in ignorance of his parentage. After the death of Uther, Arthur is the only one able to draw a sword from a magic stone and so is crowned king of Britain. With the aid of Ban and Boors, he defends his throne against eleven kings. Before he learns his parentage, he has an affair with his half-sister, Morgawse, and begets Mordred upon her. Pellynor follows the questing beast; Nyneve, the Lady of the Lake, gives Arthur a sword with a magic scabbard; Balen wounds Pellam, father of Pelleaus, and he and his brother Balan kill one another. Arthur marries Gwenyver, whose father, Lodegraunce, gives him the Table Round. Pellynor, his son Tor, and Gawayn go on separate quests. Merlin loves Nyneve, who persuades him to crawl under a stone from which he cannot extricate himself. Gawayn, Marhalt, and Ywain have further adventures.

II. *Arthur and Lucius* (Caxton v). Lucius, emperor of Rome, demands tribute from Arthur, who refuses, crosses to France, kills a giant on St. Michael's Mount, defeats Lucius, is crowned emperor by the pope, and then returns to England.

III. *Sir Launcelot* (Caxton vi). Because Launcelot surpassed all others in deeds of arms, "Queen Gwenyver had him in great favor aboven all other knights, and so he loved the Queen again aboven all other ladies." This section is a collection of mainly unconnected adventures that illustrates Launcelot's superiority in arms and his imperviousness to the blandishments of any woman other than the queen. Morgan le Fay and three other queens imprison him by enchantment and demand that he become the lover of one of them, but he refuses. He escapes; has a comic meeting with the knight Belleus; wins a tournament; kills Tarquyn and releases his prisoners, who include his nephew, Lyonell, and his brother, Ector; and meets the sorceress Hallewes, whose deadly charms he avoids.

IV. *Sir Gareth* (Caxton vii). Gareth, brother of Gawayn, is knighted by Launcelot. He goes in disguise to rescue the lady Lyones; at first scorned as a kitchen knave, he gains her admiration through knightly deeds and eventually marries her.

V. *Sir Tristram* (Caxton viii-xii). Tristram, champion of King Mark of Cornwall, is wounded by the Irish champion Marhalt, then cured by La Beal Isode; later, he overcomes her suitor, the Saracen Palomydes. He escorts Isode to Cornwall to be the bride of Mark, but on the voyage they accidentally drink a magic potion that causes them to become lovers. They escape to a forest, are discovered, and Mark carries off Isode. Tristram is wounded and cured in Brittany. After imprisonments, escapes, and a period of madness, Tristram carries La Beal Isode to England, wins a tournament, and goes with her to Launcelot's castle of Joyous Gard, where he discovers that Palomydes still loves Isode. At this point (Caxton xi), a flashback relates how Launcelot was tricked into begetting Galahad upon King Pelleaus' daughter, Elayne, who he thought was Gwenyver, and thus prepares for the Grail narrative that follows. The section ends with the reconciliation of Tristram and Palomydes. (Only by a brief aside more than two hundred pages later [Caxton xx, 6] are we informed that Tristram, under a safe conduct, returns Isode to Mark, who stabs him in the back).

VI. *The Sankgreal* (Caxton xiii-xviii). The knights of the Table Round go in quest of the Grail. Launcelot reaches the castle, but receives only a partial vision and abandons the quest because of his unworthiness. Only Percivale, Boors, and Galahad see Joseph of Aramathy use the Grail to perform a mass in which "the bread was formed of a fleshly man" [transubstantiation]. Galahad then cures the maimed King Pelleaus. The three carry the Grail to Sarras, where Galahad and Percivale die, and Boors returns to England to tell their story.

VII. *Sir Launcelot and Queen Gwenyver* (Caxton xviii-xix). After his unsuccessful quest of the Grail, Launcelot returns to the love of Gwenyver. A knight is poisoned at a banquet given by Gwenyver, and she is accused of the crime. Launcelot defends her in a trial by combat. Later, at a tournament, to disguise himself he wears the token of Elayne, the maid of Astolat. The queen thinks he loves another and is angry, but relents when the dead body of Elayne is found floating in a barge to Westminster with a letter that explains she died of unrequited love for Launcelot. Gwenyver is abducted by Mellyagaunce, and her knights are wounded; Launcelot pursues, his horse is killed, and he rides in a woodcutter's cart to rescue her. He cuts his hand on the iron bars of her window when he visits her at night. In the morning, the blood is seen, and she is accused of adultery with one of the wounded knights in her train. Launcelot successfully defends her in trial by combat. Sir Urre has wounds that only the best knight in the world can cure, so only Launcelot is able to heal him.

VIII. *The Morte Arthur* (Caxton xx-xxi). Launcelot is caught in Gwenyver's bed by Aggravayne and Mordred, and though he fights his way free, the adultery is revealed to Arthur. Gwenyver is condemned to be burned at the stake. Launcelot rescues her by force, and in the melee unintentionally kills Gaheris and Gareth, the brothers of Gawayn. He carries her to his castle of Joyous Gard, which Arthur and Gawayn besiege, but Launcelot refuses to fight his sovereign and his friend. The pope orders the restoration of Gwenyver to Arthur. Launcelot retires to Benwyk in France where Arthur and Gawayn, still bent on vengeance, besiege him. He unwillingly fights Gawayn and wounds him twice, but refuses to kill him.

While Arthur is in France, his son Mordred seizes his kingdom. Arthur lands at Dover where Gawayn is mortally wounded and sends a letter of forgiveness to Launcelot. In the final battle at Salesbury, Arthur kills Mordred but is himself mortally wounded, and his army is destroyed because he does not have Launcelot to fight for him. He tells Bedwere to cast his sword, Excaleber, into the lake, and he is carried by three ladies in a barge to Avylion. Gwenyver becomes a nun at Amesbury; when Launcelot returns to her, she says, "Never see me no more. . . for through thee and me is the flower of kings and knights destroyed." Launcelot does penance for six years as a holy hermit. Gwenyver dies and is buried beside Arthur at Glastonbury. Soon after her death, Launcelot dies, is buried at Joyous Gard, and his brother, Sir Ector, pronounces his eulogy: "Thou were never matched of earthly knight's hand. . . thou were the truest lover of a sinful man that ever loved woman, and thou were the kindest man that ever strake with sword."

ARTHUR OF LITTLE BRITAIN.

The hystory of the moost noble and valyaunt knyght Arthur of lytell brytayne, translated out of frensshe in to englushe by the noble Johan Bourghcher knyght lorde Barners, newly Imprynted, R. Redborne, c. 1555 (one or more earlier editions have been lost), c. 1582. Ed. E.V. U[tterson], 1814. About 230,000 words. Translated from the fourteenth-century French prose *Le livre du vaillant et preux chevalier Artus fils du duc de Bretagne,* Lyon, 1493, etc. Since John Bourchier, Lord Berners, calls himself "but a learner of the language of French," this is probably his first translation, done before 1523 when he published the first volume of his Froissart. He apologizes for translating "such a feigned matter, wherein seemeth to be so many unpossibilities;" but since other histories of great conquerors contain supernatural marvels, he supposes that this author "devised it not without some manner of truth or virtuous intent." A chivalric romance, not concerned with King Arthur of England.

Duke Johan of Brytayne (Brittany, Little Britain), of the lineage of Launcelot, has a son, Arthur, who is educated by Sir Governar. The young Arthur meets in the forest and falls in love with the fourteen-year-old Jehannet, but his parents force him to marry Perron. Perron's mother knows that her daughter is not a virgin, and on the wedding night she substitutes Jehannet so her daughter's lack of chastity will not be found out. Later, Jehannet confesses the deception.

Arthur, his cousin Hector, and Sir Governar go to seek adventures and come to the court of King Emendus of Soroloys and his daughter, Florence. At Florence's birth, Proserpyne, Queen of the Fairies, had prophesied that she would wed the best knight in the world who would bear a white shield and the sword Clarence. The emperor of Inde asks her hand, but she puts him off for a year. When Arthur and his friends approach, her companion Steven, who is skilled in necromancy, informs her that the knight of Proserpyne's prophecy is near.

Arthur and his friends have many adventures. He parts from Sir Governar, and with

Steven's help he gets the white shield and sword Clarence on Mount Peryllous. He rescues Sir Governar from prison, and further adventures keep him from Florence. Proserpyne tells Florence that Arthur loves her truly but that they will have to endure many troubles. Finally, King Emendus orders his daughter to marry the emperor of Inde; but at the wedding ceremony, the fairy Proserpyne takes Florence's place and vanishes at the altar.

Arthur bears Florence to Porte Noyre, where her father and the emperor besiege them. By magic, Steven bears King Emendus, asleep in his bed, to Porte Noyre, where he is reconciled to his daughter Florence. Then, while Arthur goes to Brytayne to see his old love, Jehannet, the emperor of Inde besieges Florence in Clere Toure. Arthur comes to the rescue and imprisons the emperor. Finally, Arthur marries Florence, and Sir Governar marries Jehannet. After the death of King Emendus, Arthur is crowned king of Soroloys and reigns with Florence for thirty-two years. When they die, their son, Alexander, succeeds them and afterwards becomes emperor of Inde and Constantinople.

AYMON.
The four sons of Aymon. William Caxton, c. 1489, c. 1504, 1554. Translated by Caxton from the 1480 print of the early fifteenth-century French prose *Les quatre filz Aymon,* which was adapted from the late twelfth-century metrical *Renaud de Montauban.* About 183,000 words. Ed. Octavia Richardson, EETSes 44–45, 1884-85. A romance connected with Charlemagne.

Duke Aymon of Dordon remains loyal to Charlemagne, even when the emperor attacks his brother, Duke Beuves. Charlemagne knights Aymon's four sons—Renaud, Alard, Guichard, and Richard. Renaud quarrels over a chess game with Charlemagne's nephew and kills him. With his wonderful horse, Bayard, he flees with his brothers to the forest of Ardennes where Aymon, still loyal to the emperor, fights against them. They take their cousin Maugis, who had stolen gold from Charlemagne, into their company. At Bordeaux, they free King John of Gascony; Renaud builds the castle of Montauban and marries King John's sister, Clare.

Roland proclaims a horse race for a prize at Paris. Renaud and Maugis attend in disguise, win the race with Bayard, and seize Charlemagne's crown as the prize. Roland is sent against the four sons and captures the youngest, Richard. Just as Richard is about to be hanged, Maugis, in disguise, rescues him. Oliver then captures Maugis, but he escapes and takes with him the swords of Charlemagne, Roland, and Oliver. Charlemagne besieges the sons in Montauban. The sons capture Duke Richard, and Charlemagne, to save him, offers them peace if he is given Bayard and if Renaud goes as a pilgrim to the Holy Land. When Charlemagne receives Bayard, he has him thrown into the River Meuse with a millstone around his neck, but the horse breaks the stone and gallops into the forest of Ardennes, where his neighing is still heard.

Renaud and Maugis help to free Jerusalem from the Persians. They return to France and learn that Renaud's wife has died. Charlemagne knights Renaud's two sons; Renaud then goes as a pilgrim to Cologne, where he works as a laborer on the Church of St. Peter. The other laborers are jealous of Renaud because he accomplishes more work than they do. They kill him and throw his body into the Rhine, but fish support it on the surface of the water. The laborers confess their crime, and when Renaud's body is buried, it is carried by invisible hands to the town of Croine. The archbishop has his body entombed in Cologne, where it rests to this day. He is called "St. Renaud the martyr."

BARLAM AND JOSAPHAT.

Historia Sanctorum Barlam et Iosaphat. A mid-fifteenth century Middle-English translation of the late eleventh-century "second" Latin version of the life of Josaphat, descending ultimately, with many changes, from the second-century A.D. Sanskrit *Buddhacarita,* a popular life of Buddha. Over 78,000 words. Preserved in a single manuscript, Peterhouse, Cambridge, 257, c. 1480; ed. John C. Hirsh, EETS 290, 1986. A pseudo-biography, setting forth the ascetic ideals of Christian monasticism, this story was extraordinarily popular. The "second" Latin version was disseminated in more than sixty manuscripts, was printed in 1474 and often thereafter in the *Opera* of John of Damascus, and was translated into most of the European vernaculars, including three English metrical versions. In the thirteenth century it was epitomized to less than a tenth of its original length by Vincent of Beauvais, in his *Speculum historiale,* and Jacobus de Voragine, in his *Legenda aurea* (translated into English and printed by Caxton in 1483), which cut down the long expositions of doctrine but retained eight of the apologues. From these sources descends the moral play *Everyman* (the three friends) and the caskets episode in *The Merchant of Venice.*

A king of India, Avenner, furiously persecutes Christian monks. His wise men prophesy that his son, Josaphat, will become rich and mighty, but also will become a monk. To prevent this, the king has his son brought up in a palace of pleasure where he will see no illness or adversity and gain no knowledge of Christianity. But when Josaphat arrives at young manhood, he goes out of the palace and sees a leper, a blind man, and an old man, and is depressed to learn that life is full of misery and death.

King Avenner rages when he learns of Barlam's teaching and kills all the monks he can find. On the advice of his counselor, Arachis, he has the hermit Nachor pretend to be Barlam and be defeated in disputation with his wise men. But Nachor does not go through with the deceit and is himself converted by Josaphat. The king then consults the magician Theodas, who tells the apologue of the devils who deceive men and women. The magician has the Devil send a fair damsel, who pretends to be the captive daughter of the king of Syrie, to tempt Josaphat to lust; but he resists, and Theodas himself becomes a Christian and burns his books.

Finally Avenner gives half his kingdom to his son, is converted to Christianity, becomes a hermit, and dies. Josaphat then hands the combined kingdoms over to a Christian named Barachias and goes into the desert in search of Barlam. After overcoming various temptations of the Devil, he at last finds Barlam; they live long together, Barlam dies, and after many years alone Josaphat dies. Their bodies are transported by king Barachias to a great church in India, where miracles are worked at their tomb.

God reveals Josaphat's despair to Barlam, a holy monk in the desert of Sanaar, who disguises himself as a merchant and gains access to Josaphat by means of a precious stone (the

Gospel) that has marvelous virtues but can be seen only by one not defiled by sin. In a series of interviews Barlam tells Josaphat the course of Christian history, from the creation to Moses and the incarnation and crucifixion of Christ, and urges him to give up the vanities of this world for the enduring joys of the world to come. He argues in favor of asceticism, cites the example of St. Anthony, and displays his own emaciated body. He illustrates his teachings with a series of apologues that have allegorical significance: (1) the trumpet of death; (2) the choice of four caskets; (3) the man who foolishly believes a nightingale; (4) the man in the pit (the world); (5) the three friends (riches, kinsmen, and good works); (6) the king for a year (store up riches in heaven); (7) the happy poor couple; and (8) the rich man who chooses a poor wife. Barlam teaches Josaphat the articles of the Christian faith and baptizes him. He then returns to the desert and dissuades Josaphat from following by telling him (9) the tale of the tame kid and the wild goats.

BEWARE THE CAT.
A Marvelous Hystory intituled, Beware the Cat [*by William Baldwin*]. Composed 1553. About 18,000 words. Printed by John Alde, 1570 (only a manuscript transcript survives), 1570 (fragment), 1584, and 1652 (lost). Ed. James O. Halliwell, 1864 (inaccurately from a manuscript copy of the first edition—only ten copies printed); ed. William H. Holden, 1963 (from 1584). Printed in full above.

BLANCHARDINE.
[*Blanchardine and Eglantine.*] Translation by William Caxton, 1489, from a manuscript of the fifteenth-century French prose *Blanchardine et l'orgueilleuse d'amor* (abridged from the thirteenth-century metrical romance). About 60,000 words. Printed by Caxton, Westminster, 1489 (STC 3124), ed. Leon Kellner, EETSes 58, 1890. A version considerably different in wording, purportedly translated from Latin by F.T. Goodwine, was printed in 1595 and 1597 (STC 3125-26).

Blanchardine, only son of the king of Frise, is kept from a knowledge of arms, but when he sees a tapestry depicting the wars of Troy, he takes his father's sword and steals away. He is dubbed by a wounded knight and befriended by the Knight of the Ferry, who tells him about Queen Eglantine of Tormaday who scorns love, but who is about to be besieged by King Alymodes of Norway. He meets Eglantine on the highway, kisses her, and rides on. He is befriended by the provost of Tormaday, whose daughter gives him her sleeve to wear. Eglantine finally confesses her love for Blanchardine, and they plan to be married.
    Meanwhile, King Alymodes, with his son, Darius, and daughter, Beatrice, and the giant Rubyon besiege Tormaday. Blanchardine kills Rubyon, but is himself taken prisoner, and despite the pleas of Beatrice, he is sent to Rubyon's brother. The company conveying him is shipwrecked; he escapes to Pruse, and with Sadoyne, son of the king of Pruse, captures the invading king of Poland.
    Meanwhile Darius, son of Alymodes, captures Blanchardine's father, the king of Frise, imprisons him in a dungeon in his own country of Cassydonye, and rejoins Alymodes at

the siege of Tormaday. Eglantine sends her provost to get help from Norway.

Blanchardine and Sadoyne sail to raise the siege of Tormaday. They meet the provost; a storm drives them from their course, but subsides when Sadoyne is baptized. They land in Cassydonye, the kingdom of Alymodes, where Blanchardine kills Darius and where Sadoyne marries Darius' sister, Beatrice, after she is baptized. Blanchardine frees his father, and they all sail for Tormaday, which is still besieged by Alymodes.

When they arrive at Tormaday, Alymodes captures Sadoyne and carries him off in his ship. Blanchardine puts Eglantine in the care of the low-born Subyon and sails away to rescue Sadoyne. But Subyon attacks Eglantine, who is defended by the provost and the Knight of the Ferry.

Meanwhile, Alymodes carries Sadoyne prisoner to Cassydonye, but Alymodes' daughter, Beatrice, shuts the gates against him. Sadoyne bursts his bonds and invades the city. When Blanchardine arrives, they together capture Alymodes, and Sadoyne is crowned king.

Blanchardine and Sadoyne then rescue Eglantine and execute Subyon. They return to Tormaday, where Blanchardine marries Eglantine. Sadoyne returns to his wife, Beatrice; his father, the king of Pruse, visits him and is baptized.

CASTLE OF LOVE.
The castell of love, translated out of Spanishe in to Englyshe, by Johan Bourchier knyght, lord Bernis, at the instaunce of the lady Elizabeth Carew...The whiche boke treateth of the love betwene Leriano and Laureola doughter of the kynge of Macedonia, J. Turke, c. 1549 (facsimile ed. William G. Crane, Gainesville, Fla., 1950, Scholars' Facsimiles and Reprints), c. 1550 (with verse additions by Androwe Spigurnell), c. 1560. About 34,000 words. Translated by Lord Berners before 1533 from the 1526 French translation of Lelio Manfredi's 1514 Italian translation of Diego Hernandez de San Pedro's *Cárcel del amor*, 1492; only at the end did Berners translate from the Spanish a short continuation which Nicolas Nuñez had added in 1508. A love story told in the first person by the author observer.

One morning in Macedonia, I meet a fierce knight named Desire who leads another knight prisoner who asks me to aid him. I follow them to a castle and find the knight, chained to a burning chair, who says, "I am Leriano, son of Duke Guerro; I fell in love with Laureola, daughter of King Guallo of Macedonia; this is the Castle of Love," and he then explains the allegory of the building. I go to seek out Laureola, tell her what I have seen, and ask her to pity Leriano. She replies that my request offends her virtue. Later, I speak to her again and she blushes, but "according as she showed after, she received these alterations more of pity than of love." I advise Leriano to write to her. He does, and I deliver his letter. Laureola says that she can not relieve Leriano without being defamed; but she receives the letter and writes one in reply, saying that she does not love him, but to be secret. When Leriano receives her letter, he feels cured and returns to court.

A courtier named Persius tells the king that Leriano and Laureola spend their nights together. The king imprisons his daughter and tells Persius to write a challenge. Persius is defeated by Leriano and yields, but he bribes three men to testify falsely against him. The king believes them and condemns his daughter to death. Leriano kills Persius, frees

Laureola from prison, and puts her in the care of her uncle. He then retreats to his own castle, where the king besieges him. Leriano captures one of the false witnesses, who confesses under torture. The king pardons his daughter, but orders Leriano not to return to court until he has appeased the kinsmen of Persius for his death.

Leriano writes Laureola that he will die if he does not see her. She replies that she has already suffered enough for writing to him and will never see him again. Leriano takes to his bed; his friend Tesco, to comfort him, speaks of the many evils of women. Leriano delivers a long speech in defense of women. His mother comes to visit and comfort him [here Nuñez's continuation begins], but he swallows Laureola's letter and dies.

I tell Laureola of his death, who says she would have given him any reward but her honesty. I go to my chamber, where I dream that I see Leriano and Laureola, and hear them speak together, and "knew well that Leriano received glory to see her, and Laureola received no pain to see him, though he were dead." I dream that she allows him to kiss her hand, which she had never allowed him living, and that she speaks to me and leaves sighing. Then I awake, sing a song of the sadness of love, and return to Spain, my own country.

Except for the lively account of Leriano's duel with Persius, his freeing of Laureola from prison, and his withstanding the siege, the bulk of the work consists of verbatim reports of set speeches and letters; but their style is graceful and effective, and they reveal an intricate play of emotions ranging from the passion of Leriano, through the sympathetic concern of the author, to the affectionless pity of Laureola. The author maintains his first-person point of view consistently, and his work is the best-told and most affecting love story of all that are here summarized.

CHARLES THE GREAT.
Thystory of Charles the grate Kyng of fraunce. Translated by William Caxton, 1485, from the fifteenth-century French prose *Fier a bras,* attributed to Jean Bagnyon. About 72,000 words. Ed. Sidney J.H. Herrtage, EETSes 36–37, 1880–1881. A complete life of Charlemagne, the material of Books I and III deriving from the *Speculum historiale* of Vincent of Beauvais, and of Book II from the twelfth-century French metrical *Fierabras.*

Book I. Cloys is the first Christian king of France. After his line fails, Pepyn is chosen king; his son Charles is made emperor and goes to free the Holy Land from the Turks.

Book II. Fierabras, king of Alexandria and son of the Turk Balan, admiral of Spain, challenges the French. Roland refuses to fight because Charles had praised the older knights. Oliver, against the wishes of his father, fights Fierabras and overcomes him, but is himself taken prisoner by the Saracens and is released by Balan's daughter, Floripas. Charles and Balan send messengers to one another; the French kill the Saracen messengers and send their heads to Balan; by a trick, they cross the bridge of Mantrible over the river Flagot and get to the castle of Aigremont where Balan captures and imprisons them. Balan's daughter, Floripas, for love of Guy of Burgoyne, gets the prisoners into her custody. With the help of Floripas, the messengers capture the castle and withstand a siege (aided by her magic girdle).

The besieged messengers send Richard of Normandy for help; he kills Clarion, nephew

Balan, crosses the river Flagot, and reaches Charles. The French forces kill the giant Galafre and cross the bridge of Mantrible; they overcome the scythe-wielding giantess, Amyot; her two sons are baptized. Ganelon distinguishes himself at Aigremont; Balan is captured; his daughter Floripas is baptized and marries Guy of Burgoyne.

Book III. At the bidding of St. James, Charles invades Spain. Charles vanquishes Aigoland, and Roland overcomes the giant Ferragus. The treason of Ganelon is discovered; Roland and Oliver are slain; and Ganelon is punished. Charles gives thanks to God and St. Denis, and then goes to Almayn where he dies and is buried.

COLOGNE.
The Three Kings of Cologne, W. de Worde, 1496, c. 1499, 1511, 1526, 1530 (revised by Richard Whytforde). An anonymous translation made about 1400 of John of Hildesheim's Latin *Historia trium regum* (composed 1364–1375). About 28,000 words. Preserved in ten fifteenth-century MSS, ed. C. Horstmann, EETSes 85, 1886.

The first half tells, with considerable elaboration, the biblical story of the visit of the Magi (Melchior of Nubia, Balthasar of India, and Jaspar of Ethiopia) to the infant Jesus, their gifts of gold, incense, and myrrh, and their return to their own countries by another route. The second half tells later episodes in the life of the Virgin Mary, the history of the thirty gilt pennies from Abraham to Judas, the baptism of the Three Kings by St. Thomas of India, their deaths, their successor (Prester John), and the translation of their bodies, first to Constantinople by St. Helena, next to Milan by St. Eustorgius, and finally to Cologne (in 1164). The narrative is supplemented by numerous descriptions of places, customs, and sects—a compilation of all that was then known about the marvels of the East, taking up more than half of the book.

DESTRUCTION OF JERUSALEM.
The dystruccyon of Jherusalem by Vaspazyan and Tytus, R. Pynson, c. 1508, c. 1513, 1528. About 22,000 words. Anonymous translation of the French prose *La destruction de Jherusalem et la mort de pilate,* Lyons, c. 1485. A religious fictionalizing of history.

Forty years after the crucifixion, the emperor of Rome, Vaspazyan, suffers from a disease that no physician can cure. His seneschal, Guy, tells him that anything that has touched the prophet Jhesu will cure him. The emperor sends Guy to Jerusalem, where he is told of the miracle of Veronica's veil. Guy returns with Veronica, Vaspazyan is cured, and he vows to avenge the death of Jhesu by destroying the Jews. With his son, Tytus, he besieges Jerusalem. There is no food in the city, and the inhabitants eat the leather from the gates. The sons of Queen Mary of Africa and her friend Claryce both die of starvation, so the women eat their sons to fulfill the prophecy of Christ that the mother shall eat her child for hunger. The Jews surrender unconditionally, and 73,350 of them are slaughtered, all but thirty of whom are sold for a penny each. The conquerors return to Rome where Vaspazyan, Tytus, Joseph of Armathye, and others are baptized by Clement. Pylate is sent

to Vyenee, where he is placed in a tower and lingeringly tortured for twenty-one days, at
the end of which time devils cry out, "Pylate is ours," and the tower sinks beneath the river.
    For another prose account, see A. Kurvinen, *Memoires de la Société Neophilologique
de Helsinki,* 34 (1969).

DESTRUCTION OF TROY.
*The faythfull and true storye of the destruction of Troye, compyled by Dares Phrygius, which
was a souldier while the siege lasted. Translated into Englyshe by Thomas Paynell,* 1553.
Translated from the French translation by Mathurin Heret (Paris, 1553) of Dares' sixth-century
Latin *De excidio Trojae historia.* About 17,500 words.

    Jason, on his voyage for the golden fleece, is refused hospitality at Troy by Laomedon.
Later Hercules, to avenge the insult done his friend, sacks Troy and kills Laomedon, and
his companion Thelamon carries off Laomedon's daughter, Hesiona. Priamus, Laomedon's
son, rebuilds Troy and demands that the Greeks return his sister. When they refuse, his
son Alexander leads an expedition into Greece where he meets Helena, wife of Menelaus,
and brings her back with him to Troy.
    Agamemnon, brother of Menelaus, leads a Greek force against Troy. Achilles kills Hector
and then falls in love with Hector's sister, Polixena. He at first stays away from battle because
of his love for Polixena but when many of his men are killed, he enters the fight and kills
Troilus. Alexander then ambushes and kills Achilles, and Ajax kills Alexander. Penthesilea
comes with her Amazons to aide the Trojans, and she is killed by Neoptolemus, son
of Achilles.
    After ten years' war, Antenor and Eneas suggest that the Trojans sue for peace, but Pri-
amus refuses. So Antenor and Eneas enter into secret negotiations with the Greeks and finally
let them into the city through a gate that has a horse's head carved on it. The Greeks sack
Troy; Neoptolemus kills Priamus at the altar of Jupiter and slits Polixena's throat on the
tomb of his father, Achilles. The traitors Antenor and Eneas and their families are spared.
There then follows "Menelaus' oration unto the Troyanes," a formal speech of twenty-three
pages [not in the Latin text], arguing that the Greeks were justified in waging war on Troy.

EULENSPIEGEL, see HOWLEGLAS.

EURIALUS AND LUCRECE.
*The goodli history of the moste noble and beautyful Ladye Lucres of Scene in Tuskane, and
of her lover Eurialus.* J. Van-Doesborch, 1515(?), 1553(?), 1560, 1567; ed. H.H. Gibbs in
his *Hystorie of Plasidas,* 1873 (Roxburghe Club). About 19,000 words. An anonymous translation of the Latin *De duobus amantibus Eurialo et Lucresia,* composed in 1444 by Enea
Silvio Piccolomini (later Pope Pius II), which was printed sixty-two times by 1500.

    When the Emperor Sygismonde enters Scene (Siena), Eurialus, a thirty-two-year-old gentleman in his train, sees the fair Lucrece, who is under twenty and married to a citizen named Menelaus. He falls in love with her, and she falls in love with him. Eurialus sends her a letter; she tears it up, but when her servant leaves she puts the pieces together and reads them. She sends Eurialus a ring as repayment for his gifts. Her manservant, Zosias, remonstrates with her, but finally decides to help further her romance because, "If chastity cannot be kept, it is enough to hide the noise." They exchange letters and take every opportunity to see one another. When her husband goes away, Eurialus visits her; but when Menelaus unexpectedly returns, he hides in a closet, and Lucrece dumps a casket of jewels out of the window to distract her husband from going to the closet.

Another knight, Pacorus, also courts Lucrece, but she ignores him. Eurialus hides in the stable in order to gain access to Lucrece and is almost pitchforked by the ostler. The two lovers hold a passionate conversation through a door they can only half open. Finally, Eurialus has to go to Rome with the emperor. Lucrece sickens and dies. Eurialus follows the emperor through many countries, finally hears of the death of Lucrece, and grieves ever after, even though the emperor gives him a noble lady as his wife.

The appeal of the work is to sentiment through a humanistic style. Nine eloquent letters and several conversations are reported. The names of the characters are all classical—Lucrece is unfaithful to her husband, Menelaus, who has a brother, Agamemnon; Eurialus has a friend named Nisus. (In all of Malory, there are only two classical references—to Hector and Alexander as mighty warriors).

HELYAS.
Helyas knyght of the swanne. W. de Worde, 1512, c. 1550, ed. R[obert] H[oe], New York, 1901 (Grolier Club); modernized by H. Morley, *Early Prose Romances,* 1889. Translation by Robert Copland, 1512, of Pierre Desrey's French prose *La généalogie avecques les gestes...du...Goddefroy de Boulion et de ses...frères Baudoin et Eustace...descendus ...du...chevalier au Cyne* (Paris, 1504, derived from the late twelfth-century metrical *Hélias chevalier au Cygne*). About 35,000 words. The fictionalized ancestry of the historical Godfrey of Bouillon, king of Jerusalem (d. 1100).

Pyeron of Lylefort marries Matabrune, who bears him a son named Oryant. Oryant marries Beatryce, who at one birth has six sons and a daughter, each with a silver chain about its neck. The evil Matabrune orders a servant to kill her daughter-in-law's children, but the servant leaves them in a forest where they are found by a hermit. Matabrune learns that the children are still alive and sends a huntsman to kill them. The huntsman finds only six of the children (young Helyas was with the hermit), but instead of killing them takes their silver chains; when he does so, they turn into swans. Matabrune gives the chains to a goldsmith with orders to make them into a cup, but he melts only one of them and keeps the other five.

Matabrune causes the false knight Makayre to report that Beatryce has coupled with a dog and given birth to seven puppies. An angel reveals her plot. Helyas overcomes Makayre, who confesses and is hanged; he then burns Matabrune to death in her castle. The five silver chains are obtained from the goldsmith, and five of the swans are restored to human form—

but the sixth remains a swan. Helyas, guided by his swan brother, sails to Nymaie and then to Boulyon, where he kills an earl who is oppressing the duchess. He marries the daughter of the duchess, but refuses to tell her from what country he came. She bears him a daughter, Ydain. After seven years, Helyas brings his wife and daughter in the ship of his swan brother to Nymaie and places them in the care of the emperor, Otton.

Helyas returns to Lylefort where his parents, Oryant and Beatryce, welcome him. They get the silver cup from the goldsmith and have it made into two chalices. By divine intervention, his swan brother is restored to human shape and baptized. Helyas then becomes a religious hermit. When his daughter, Ydain, reaches the age of thirteen, she marries Eustace, earl of Boulyon. She dreams that she will bear three children, who would free Jerusalem from the Saracens, and in the three following years she bears Godfrey of Boulyon, Baudwyn, and Eustace.

Helyas' wife, who becomes duchess of Boulyon after the death of her mother, sends her squire, Ponce, to seek her husband. Ponce goes by way of Jerusalem and Rome to the new castle of Boulyon that Helyas had built. Helyas, who has remained as a holy hermit, gives Ponce a ring to bring to his wife.

Ydain brings up her sons in virtue; and when the eldest, Godfrey, is fifteen, he is knighted by the emperor. Then comes the time when God had ordained that Jerusalem would be freed from the "paynyms" by Godfrey.

HOWLEGLAS.

A merye Jest of a man that was called Howleglas. An anonymous translation of an abbreviated version of the German *Tyl Ulenspiegel,* 1515 *(Till Eulenspiegel),* of about 28,000 words in 47 chapters (the German has 96), printed at Antwerp c. 1519 and reprinted three times in London by c. 1565. The fragmentary first edition was edited by Friedrich Brie in his *Eulenspiegel in England,* Berlin, 1903; a bowdlerized version was edited by K. R. H. Mackenzie, London, 1860; and the full text by Frederic Ouvry, London, 1867, and P.M. Zall in his *Hundred Merry Tales and Other Jestbooks,* Lincoln, Nebraska, 1963 (with a few deletions).

This is a jestbook biography of unconnected anecdotes, many of them scatalogical, which show up the selfish motives and subterfuges of citizens and churchmen. Howleglas is born in a small German village. When he is christened, he is accidentally dropped in the mud on the way home and then washed in warm water; so he is "three times in one day christened—once at the church, once in the mud, and once in the warm water" (chap. 1). He is hired by an earl to paint portraits of his ancestors on a wall of his palace. He actually paints nothing, but before exhibiting his blank wall he tells the earl and his courtiers that "he the which is not born in wedlock may not see my painting"; so all pretend they see paintings and praise his work (chap. 18). A parson keeps a maid as a concubine; Howleglas makes his confession to the parson and tells him he has lain with his maid; the parson then accuses his maid of unfaithfulness and beats her; whereupon Howleglas blackmails the parson because he had revealed his confession (chap. 24). He is ordered by an abbot to count how many of his monks attend matins. He removes part of the stairs, so that the first monk who descends to attend matins falls and breaks his leg, and the rest come tumbling after him. When the abbot berates him, Howleglas says he has counted the monks: "here is the tally" (chap. 41). He even plays a scatalogical trick on the priest who comes to administer him the last rites (chap. 45); and when he is lowered into his grave, the coffin falls in upright, so he is buried that way (chap. 47).

HUON OF BORDEAUX.

The boke of duke Huon of burdeaux and of them that issuyd fro him, c. 1534 (lost), 1570 (lost), and 1601. Translation by Sir John Bourchier, Lord Berners, c. 1530, of the French *Les prouesses et faitz merveilleux du noble Huon de bordeaux,* Paris, 1513, compiled c. 1434 from the thirteenth-century chanson de geste. About 234,000 words in 194 chapters. Ed. Sidney L. Lee, EETSes 40-41, 43, 50, 1882-1887. A chivalric romance loosely connected with the Charlemagne cycle.

I, 1-85 *Huon.* In the year 756, after the battle of Roncesvalles, Charles the Great summons to his court Huon, son of the deceased Duke Seuyn of Bordeaux. On his way to court, Huon is ambushed by Charlot, the king's son, and in self-defense kills him. In revenge, Charles orders Huon to perform an impossible task: to bring from Babylon the beard and four teeth of the Admiral Gaudyse and to kiss his daughter, Esclaramond.

Near Jerusalem, Huon meets the dwarf Oberon, son of Julius Caesar and king of the fairies, who gives him a cup that will always be full and a horn that will always summon aid, but warns him, "Thou shalt suffer by thine own folly." The bearman Malabron, sent by Oberon, helps Huon on his journey and warns him never to tell a lie. He gets to Babylon, gains entrance to the castle of Gaudys by saying he is a Saracen, and kisses Esclaramond. He is imprisoned by Gaudys, and Oberon refuses to aid him because he has lied. Old Gerames comes to his rescue, and with the help of Oberon, who has relented, Gaudys is slain and Huon takes his beard and teeth.

Huon sails away with Esclaramond, but they are shipwrecked on a desert island, where she is carried off by pirates and taken from them by the giant Galaffer. Malabron transports Huon to the mainland, where the minstrel Mouflet brings him to the castle of Ivroyn, brother of Gaudys, who orders him to play chess with his daughter and be killed if he loses. The daughter falls in love with Huon and saves his life by losing to him. Huon aids Ivroyn in an attack on Galaffer, who, unbeknown to him, has been joined by Gerames. Huon and Gerames fight, but recognize one another, and Galaffer submits to Ivroyn. Then news comes that Huon's brother Gerard has seized his lands. He sails for France, and on the way is married to Esclaramond by the pope at Rome.

Huon arrives at Bordeaux and generously offers his brother part of his lands, but the brother casts him into a dungeon, gets possession of the beard and teeth of Gaudys, and tells King Charles that Huon had not accomplished the task set for him. The good Duke Naymes, with the help of Oberon, reveals the treachery of Gerard, who is hanged. Oberon restores the beard and teeth to Huon, who presents them to Charles and is pardoned. Oberon tells Huon to come in four years to Mommure to succeed him as king of the fairies.

II, 86-157 *Huon and Esclaramond.* Oberon predicts more suffering for Huon, who falls out of the emperor's favor and is besieged in Bordeaux. Esclaramond bears a daughter,

Claryet, and Huon leaves Bordeaux to get help from her brother, Salybraunt. He sails over the Perilous Gulf, where he meets Judas, and journeys to the castle of Adamant, where he kills a serpent and is fed by fairies. He is carried from the castle by a griffin, an angel tells him to pick three magical apples, and he sails for Persia.

Meanwhile, Esclaramond yields Bordeaux to the emperor, is imprisoned in Magence, and sends Sir Barnard to take her daughter to safety with the abbot of Cluney (with help from Huon). Sir Barnard finds Huon in Persia; after helping the admiral of Persia against the sultan of Babylon, they return to France. The emperor is about to burn Esclaramond at the stake when she is rescued by Oberon. Huon and his wife are finally reconciled with the emperor, to whom he gives the apple of youth. Huon then goes to Fairyland to succeed Oberon, where the throne is for a time contested by King Arthur, who later withdraws.

III, 158–173 *Claryet.* Claryet, daughter of Huon and Esclaramond, marries Florent, prince of Aragon, and dies giving birth to a daughter, Ide.

IV, 174–180 *Ide.* When Ide is fifteen, her father tries to seduce her; to escape him, she disguises herself as a man and goes to Rome. Olive, the daughter of the emperor, falls in love with her and marries her. She confesses her sex to Olive, but a servant overhears and tells the emperor, who vows that both shall be burned at the stake if Ide is found to be a woman. Ide prays to the Virgin, her sex is changed, and Olive bears a son, Croysant.

V, 181–194 *Croysant.* Croysant is so liberal that he gives away all his treasure, with the result that after the death of his father, Ide, the Romans ask Guymart to rule them. Croysant goes to Nice, where after various adventures he returns to Rome. Most of his friends reject him, but two knights and Guymart help him. He marries the daughter of Guymart, after whose death he becomes emperor.

IMAGE OF GOVERNANCE.
The Image of Governance Compiled of the Actes and Sentences notable, of the most noble Emperour Alexander Severus, late translated out of Greke into Englyshe, by syr Thomas Eliot, T. Bertholet, 1540, 1544, 1549, 1556; facsimile ed. Lillian Gottesman in her *Four Political Treatises by Sir Thomas Elyot,* Fayetteville, Fla., 1967 (Scholars' Facsimiles and Reprints). About 66,000 words.

In his preface, Elyot says he translated this text about nine years ago from a book in Greek which had been written by the emperor's secretary, Eucolpius. Some of the details are from the Latin life of Severus Alexander by Aelius Lampridius (who cites "Encolpius" as one of his authorities) in the fourth-century *Historia Augusta,* a work of minimal historical authenticity; but most are the invention of Elyot himself. It is a fictional biography portraying Elyot's notion of the ideal ruler of a perfect state (an autocrat who controls his administrators by secret informers and cruel punishments and who forces his subjects to conform in their private lives to his own rigid notions of morality). The book opens with an account of Alexander's birth and closes with his death, but there is no connected account of the events of his reign. There are a few anecdotes, some letters, and many speeches illustrating principles of political action. Alexander condemns the counselor Vetronius Turinus, who accepted bribes for exerting infuence he did not have, to be smothered in smoke—

"with fume shall he die, that fumes hath sold." He writes to Gordian, saying that a ruler should not be distant from his people, and to Alexander, bishop of Alexandria, inviting Origen to Rome. He delivers speeches on the value of severe punishments, on the incommodities of marriage, and on the importance of maintaining class distinctions. There are more "sentences" than "acts" in this pseudo-biography, for it contains hardly a trace of narrative.

IMAGE OF IDLENESS.
A lyttle treatyse called the Image of Idlenesse, conteynynge certeyn matters moved betwene Walter Wedlock and Bawdin Bachelor. Translated out of the Troyane or Cornyshe tounge into Englyshe, by Olyver Oldwanton, and dedicated to the Lady Lust. Printed for William Seres, c. 1555; four editions by 1581. About 20,000 words. Though this purports to be a translation, it is an original composition (the pretence that it is translated from "Cornyshe," which suggests the horn of cuckoldry, is part of the fiction). It is told entirely in the form of letters and is therefore the first English epistolary novel.

A letter by Bawdin Bachelor to his friend Walter Wedlock describing his unsuccessful attempts at courtship and his opinions on matrimony and women, enclosing nine other letters he had written and one he had received. He writes to a friend that he has decided to marry in order to provide an example to husbands of how wives should be ruled, and he asks his friend to present his suit to a recent widow. When the widow refuses him, he sends her an epitaph for the tomb of her late husband. He writes to other women, telling stories of how Venus has punished those who do not obey her behests. One woman had promised to meet him, but did not keep the assignation; he consoles himself with the reflection that "the pastime of wooing is better than the penance of wedding." He had made a list of eleven eligible maidens and widows, and so far he has been refused by seven of them. He becomes a soldier and asks a friend of his to acquaint him with his women friends. His friend replies that his women "promise to do their best for your speed elsewhere, so it be not on any of their friends."
Since he has been unable to persuade any woman to marry him, he decides to write out his advice to husbands. A husband should use policy and pretend that he wants the opposite of what he really desires; he should "make as though he would leap out at the chamber window," but he should "let not her be too near at hand lest she happen to help him onward." He gives an example of women's "instability" by telling a long story of a gentleman who tries to seduce a gentlewoman at an inn, but always arrives at the wrong time and is superseded by another lover (later, he inadvertently reveals that he is himself the unsuccessful seducer). He concludes that, since all women are unfaithful, the best thing for husbands to do is to pretend ignorance of their misdoings, like the blacksmith who found his wife in bed with another man, but who did not reveal what he had seen, and was only glad that it was not a stranger who had seen them and so had "shamed me forever."

IPOMEDON.

Ipomedon. An anonymous prose epitome of about 17,000 words, one-third the length of the original, made c. 1460 of Hue de Rotelande's Anglo-Norman poem *Ipomédon,* composed about 1190. One MS, ed. Eugen Kölbing, *Ipomedon in drei englische Bearbeitungen,* Breslau, 1889 (with two earlier Middle-English verse translations—the couplet version was edited by Robert Copland and printed by Wynkyn de Worde, c. 1505). A chivalric romance not concerned with any of the three main "matters."

Ipomedon, prince of Poile (Apulia), visits the lady of Calabre (Calabria), who has just succeeded to the throne and who vows she will marry only the worthiest knight in all the world. The lady falls in love with him, even though he pretends to be interested in hunting rather than in marital affairs. She proclaims a three-day tournament and promises to marry the winner. Ipomedon takes part in disguise—first in white, then in red, and finally in black armor—and wins each day. He reveals his identity to the lady's servant and rides off, but promises to return at a later time.

He seeks further adventures, aiding the king of France against his vassals. Meanwhile Leonyn, a giant of India, besieges the lady of Calabre, who sends her maidservant, Emain, to seek a champion to defend her. Ipomedon disguises himself as a fool and undertakes to be the lady's champion, but Emain scorns him. He overcomes three giants, brothers of Leonyn, and Emain falls in love with him, but he refuses her advances. Ipomedon, in black armor, fights and overcomes Leonyn, who is also in black armor, so that the lady cannot tell who is the victor. Ipomedon pretends that it is Leonyn who has won, and the lady flees from him in a ship. At this time, Capaneus of Cecile (Sicily) comes to Calabre and fights Ipomedon, who still pretends to be Leonyn; but, by means of a ring, they recognize one another as half-brothers and are reconciled. Finally, Ipomedon is united with the lady of Calabre.

JASON.

The Historie of Jason Touching the Conqueste of the Golden Flese, W. Caxton [1477], Antwerp, 1492; ed. John Munro, EETSes 111, 1913. About 91,000 words. Translation by Caxton of Raoul Le Fèvre's French prose *Les fais et proesses du noble et vaillant chevalier Jason,* Bruges, 1476 (printed by Caxton), written in the early 1460s. Classical myths told in the manner of Burgundian romances of chivalry. In his prologue, Caxton says he translates this separate book because the story had been treated only briefly in his earlier *Recuyell of the histories of Troy.* Most of the episodes concerning Medea and some concerning Hypsipyle are found in classical sources, but the enveloping romance of Myrro is a new invention by Le Fèvre.

Jason, eighteen-year-old son of the elderly King Eson of Myrmidone, attends with his uncle Peleus a tournament in Thebes where he fights Hercules to a standstill. Hercules becomes his friend, but Peleus is jealous of his fame. Myrro, queen of Oliferne, is besieged by the king of Sklavonye. Jason defeats the king and his champion, the giant Corfus. He expresses his love for Myrro, but she pretends to refuse him; he leaves and she follows; they meet in Athens and agree to marry later in Oliferne. Then Jason, with Peleus and his friends Mopsius and Theseus, returns to Myrmidone.

Peleus learns from an oracle that a man with one foot bare will rule Myrmidone, and he meets Jason, who is wearing only one sandal. In order to reserve the succession to himself, he persuades Jason to undertake the dangerous quest for the golden fleece in Colchos. Argos builds a ship, and Jason sails with a hundred knights who include Hercules, Theseus, and Mopsius. They land near Troy, but the king, Laomedon, refuses them hospitality, ''so evil fell upon him afterward . . . as it shall be declared.'' They sail to Lemnos, where the queen of the Amazons, Ysiphyle (Hypsipyle), falls in love with Jason and comes to his bed even though he protests he is promised to Myrro.

After four months, they sail to Colchos, which had been founded by Apollo, where the golden fleece is guarded by a dragon. The daughter of King Oetes, the enchantress Medea, falls in love with Jason and offers to tell him how to gain the fleece if he will marry her instead of Myrro; under the influence of a magic spell, he agrees. With her ointments and instructions, he subdues the fire-breathing bulls, kills the dragon, sows its teeth, and gets the warriors who grow from them to kill one another. Medea's father refuses to allow Medea to marry Jason, so they flee together, and she slows her father's pursuit by dismembering her brother, Absirthius, and throwing the pieces behind them. As they approach Lemnos, Medea turns their ship around. Ysiphyle sees it turn, thinks Jason is deliberately deserting her, and drowns herself.

Jason return to Myrmydone and marries Medea. Hercules prepares a fleet to attack Troy. Medea, by her magic, makes Jason's father, Eson, young again. Jason's evil uncle Peleus also wants to be rejuvenated, but Medea tricks and kills him. Jason is horrified at her murder of Peleus and renounces Medea's company. He goes to Corinth, where he marries Creusa; she is killed by Medea. He then marries Myrro. His father, angry because he did not assist the expedition against Troy, besieges him in Oliferne. Medea comes to Oliferne, but Jason rejects her and kills her son. She goes to Athens and marries King Egeus; she is accused of trying to poison Theseus and takes refuge in Thessaly.

Meanwhile, Eson besieges Jason for many months in Oliferne. Then Myrro is killed by an arrow, and Jason gives up the defense of the city. He wanders to Thessaly, where he meets Medea and takes her back as his wife (after she swears never to use magic again). They are reconciled to Eson and, after his death, rule long and have many children.

Caxton adds that he has read in Boccaccio, *De genealogia deorum* XIII, that they restored Medea's father, Oetes, to his throne, and that Jason by Ysiphyle had two sons, Thoant and Euneus, who fought with Adrastus at Thebes.

MELUSINE.
Melusine. W. de Worde, c. 1510 (fragment). An anonymous translation, c. 1500, of the French prose *Melusine*, Geneva, 1478, composed by Jean d'Arras, c. 1387. About 125,000 words in sixty-two chapters. One MS ed. A.K. Donald, EETSes 68, 1895. A family romance about the imaginary ancestors of the house of Lusignan.

Elynas, king of Albany (Scotland), marries the fairy Pressyne, who makes him promise never to look at her in childbed. She bears triplets (Melusine, Melior, and Palatine); Elynas observes her, and she vanishes. The daughters, led by Melusine, imprison their father in a mountain in Northumberland. Their mother condemns Melusine to be turned into a serpent every Saturday, Melior to be keeper of a sparrowhawk, and Palatine to watch over the treasure of her father until she is released by one of her own kin.

Henry of Leon, seneschal of the king of Bretayne, is exiled, marries the daughter of the duke of Poiters, and has a son, Raymondin. Raymondin meets and marries Melusine, who makes him promise never to look at her on a Saturday. They have ten children, all but the seventh of whom has some physical defect: Urian, Odon, Guion, Anthony, Raynald, Geffray, Froymond, Horrible, Raymond, and Theodoric. Urian marries the daughter of the king of Cyprus and succeeds him as king. Guion marries the daughter of the king of Armenia and succeeds him as king. Anthony aids Christine of Luxembourgh and marries her. Raynald marries Eglantyne, daughter of the king of Behayne (Bohemia). Geffray with the Great Tooth fights the Saracens at Jaffa and Beyrouth, then returns home to fight the giant Guedon.

Meanwhile Raymondin, urged on by his brother, the earl of Forests, spies on Melusine on a Saturday and sees her in her bath as half-serpent and half-woman, but he does not tell what he has seen. His son Froymond becomes a monk, and his son Geffray in a rage kills Froymond and all the other monks in his monastery. When Raymondin learns that one of his sons has killed another, he thinks it is the work of spirits and cries out against Melusine, "Go thou hence false serpent." Melusine, in the form of a serpent, flies to Lusignan, and Raymondin grieves ever afterwards. Her son Horrible, who was of a vicious disposition and had killed his nurses, is put to death.

Geffray kills the giant Grymauld and finds the tomb of King Elynas in Northumberland. Later, his brother Raymond tells him that King Elynas was his grandfather. Geffray is reconciled to his father, Raymondin, and both confess their sins to the pope. Every year Geffray and his brother Theodoric visit their father; but one day, as they approach Lusignan, they see a serpent on the battlements, and when they reach the castle they find Raymondin dead.

The eight surviving sons of Raymondin and Melusine reign nobly and long. After the death of Guion, the last of them, one of his descendants comes to a castle where a lady keeps a sparrowhawk. She is Melior, who tells him about his ancestors and predicts the decay of his line. Here I, Jean d'Arras, finish the chronicle of the fortress of Lusignan, which has lately been conquered by John, Duke of Berry, at whose command I have collected these chronicles.

MERLIN.

[*Merlin, or the Early History of King Arthur.*] An anonymous translation, c. 1450, of the French Vulgate prose *L'estoire de Merlin,* mid-thirteenth century. About 280,000 words. Three MSS. Ed. Henry B. Wheatley, with introduction by Edward Mead, EETSes 10, 21, 36, 112, 1865–1899. The whole life of Merlin and the early life of King Arthur to the conclusion of his first campaign in Gaul.

Merlin is begotten by a devil upon a mortal woman, but is baptized by the hermit Blase and so does not become evil. While still a child, he tells Vortigern of the white and red dragons beneath his tower, and when Uter succeeds to the throne, he advises him to build the Round Table at Cardoell in Wales. He disguises Uter, and so enables him to beget Arthur upon the duke of Tintagel's wife, Ygerne. When Uter dies, a sword is seen fixed in an anvil, which only Arthur can draw out, so he is chosen king and rules all Logres (England). Arthur's half sister was the wife of King Lot, to whom she bore Gawain, Agravayn, Gaharet, and Gaheries; before Arthur became king, he lay with her without her knowledge and begot upon her Mordred. Some adventures of Gawain are told. Merlin meets Nimiane, who promises him her love if he will teach her his magic.

Arthur marries Gonnore, daughter of King Leodegan, and finally defeats the Saxons. King Ban goes to the castle of Agravadain where, with the help of Merlin's enchantments, he spends the night with his host's daughter. Merlin visits Nimiane at Benoyk and teaches her his magic arts. Arthur celebrates his victory over the Saxons by a feast at Camelot; during the feast, messengers come from Luce, emperor of Rome, demanding tribute. Arthur sails to make war on Rome, and on the way he kills a giant at St. Michael's Mount, defeats the emperor at Osten, kills a giant cat, and returns to Benoyk. Merlin takes leave of Arthur and goes to Nimiane, who asks him to teach her how to shut a person in a tower by enchantment. He says, "I know well what ye think, and that ye will me with-hold, and I am so surprised by love that me behoveth to do your pleasure." So he teaches her the enchantment, and in the forest of Brochelon, Nimiane encloses him in a fair tower: "Ne never after come Merlin out of that fortress that she had him in set." Gawain goes in search of Merlin, and Agravadain's daughter bears King Ban a son named Lancelot.

OLYVER OF CASTYLLE.
The hystorye of Olyver of Castylle and of the fayre Helayne doughter unto the kynge of Englande, W. de Worde, 1518; ed. Robert E. Graves, 1898 (Roxburghe Club); ed. Gail Orgelfinger, 1986. About 78,000 words in seventy-six chapters and an epilogue. Translated by Henry Watson from Philippe Camus' mid-fifteenth-century French prose *Le livre de olivier de castille et de artus dalgarbe son tresloyal compaignon,* Geneva, 1482. Camus said that he translated "de latin en francoys,"; but no Latin text is known, and Camus was probably the author of the French. A chivalric romance combining the themes of the Grateful Dead and the Two Friends.

At a time after the reign of Charlemagne, the queen of Castylle dies giving birth to a son who is christened Olyver. The king of Castylle then marries the widow of the deceased king of Algarbe, who has a son named Arthur—of the same age as and almost identical in appearance to Olyver. The two boys are brought up together and become fast friends. When they reach their teens, the queen declares her love for her stepson, Olyver, who flees from the court, leaving his friend Arthur a glass that will become cloudy when he falls into trouble. He joins an English knight, Sir John Talbot, and they are shipwrecked on the coast of England. Talbot is carried to Canterbury, where he dies, but his body is refused Christian burial because he owes a debt. Olyver pays the debt and has him properly buried.

Olyver hears that the king of England has proclaimed a tournament and has promised the winner his daughter, Helayne. A White Knight mysteriously appears and offers to provide Olyver equipment and servants if he will promise to give him half of what he wins. Olyver promises, wins the tournament, and after a year marries Helayne. She bears him a son, Henry, and a daughter, Charyse. In the tournament, Olyver had killed a king of Ireland, in consequence of which he is himself captured and carried prisoner to Ireland.

At this time, Arthur notices that the glass his friend had left him has become cloudy, so he goes to seek Olyver. He is shipwrecked on the coast of Ireland, where the White Knight appears and tells him to go to England and pretend to be Olyver in order to cure his wife, Helayne, of her deadly melancholy. Helayne thinks he is Olyver, but he refuses to have intercourse with her on the pretence that he had made a vow first to go on pilgrimage to Compostella. When Helayne is recovered, the White Knight leads Arthur to Olyver, whom he frees from prison. He tells Olyver of his visit to England, and Olyver thinks he has lain with his wife and throws him from his horse. Olyver later learns the truth, and the two friends are reconciled.

Arthur becomes ill, and Olyver is told in a dream that he must give his friend the blood of his own son and daughter to cure him. He beheads his children and cures Arthur by giving him their blood. Later, he finds his children alive. Then the White Knight appears and demands half of what Olyver has won according to his promise—his son and half of his wife. Olyver tearfully gives him his son and is about to cut his wife in half, when the Knight reveals that he is the soul of Sir John Talbot and pardons his debt (because by the burial Olyver had provided him, he is assured of paradise).

Olyver's daughter marries Arthur, and his son dies fighting the Saracens. After the death of Olyver and Helayne, his friend Arthur reigns as king of England, Castylle, and Algarbe. In the epilogue, the author explains that the apparent impossibilities of the action are either natural or acts of God. The narrative is wordy and slow moving, with many soliloquies, speeches, and descriptions, and the author continually comments on the action.

OVID'S METAMORPHOSES.
Ovyde hys booke of Methamorphose. Translated by W. Caxton, 1480, from a manuscript of a fifteenth-century French prose adaptation of Petrus Berchorius' fourteenth-century Latin prose *Ovidius Moralisatus.* About 220,000 words in fifteen books, preserved in a manuscript in the Pepysian Library, Cambridge, the first part of which was discovered as recently as 1966. If printed, no copy survives. Books 10–15 ed. G. Hibbert, 1819 (Roxburghe Club), and S. Gaselee and H. F. B. Brett-Smith, Oxford, 1924; Books 1–15 issued in facsimile by G. Braziller, New York, 1968.

After an introduction praising poetry, because "whoso can discover and take away the veil or shadow from the fables, he shall see clearly sometime. . . right high philosophy,'' the stories of the *Metamorphoses* are retold in Ovid's order, expanded with details from other sources with moral interpretations added. In the first book, the world is created out of chaos; the four ages of gold, silver, bronze, and iron succeed; in the following books, the giants pile Pelion on Ossa and make war on heaven until Jove destroys them; Lycaon tries to feed human flesh to Jove, who overwhelms the earth with a flood from which only Deucalion and Pyrrha escape; then come stories of Python, Apollo and Daphne, Io, and Pan and Syrinx.

In the following books, the major Greek and Roman myths are related—not chronologically, but by various associational links: Phaethon, Coronis, Europa; Actaeon, Narcissus; Pyramus and Thisbe, Mars and Venus, Salmacis and Hermaphroditus; the Muses; Arachne, Niobe, Philomela; Jason and Medea; Daedalus and Icarus; Hercules; Orpheus and Eurydice; Bacchus; and Ceyx and Alcyone. The last four books tell of the Trojan War, the wanderings of Ulysses, the founding of Rome by Aeneas, and the metamorphosis of Julius Caesar into a star. World history, from the creation to Ovid's own time, is presented in an intricately woven web of myths. The appended interpretations of the myths stress their moral rather than their doctrinal implications. Thus Lycaon, instead of being presented as a type of Satan as in Berchorius, is said to have been "transformed and turned into a wolf forsomuch as he exercised more the condition of a wolf than of a human creature."

PARIS AND VIENNE.

Thystorye of the noble knyght Parys and of the fayr Vyenne, W. Caxton, 1485, 1492, c. 1505; revised by M. Mainwaringe [1628], [1632?], 1650. Ed. MacEdward Leach, EETSes 234, 1957. About 26,000 words. Translated by Caxton from a manuscript of the French prose *Paris et Vienne,* after 1432.

In the year 1271, Vienne, the fifteen-year-old daughter of the dauphin, and her companion, Isabel, live in the city of Vienne, where also live the eighteen-year-old Paris and his friend Edward. Paris loves Vienne, but because she is superior to him in rank, he dares not tell her. He enters tournaments in disguise as her champion and wins. Vienne falls in love with her champion, but does not know who he is. While he is absent, Vienne visits his castle and sees in his room the trophies he had won at the tournaments; when he returns, she declares her love for him.

At Vienne's urging, Paris asks her father for her hand, but the great nobleman haughtily refuses. Vienne then asks Paris to elope with her, and in man's attire she flees with him toward the seacoast. A storm arises; they cannot proceed because the rivers are flooded, and the dauphin's servants are in close pursuit. Paris, in remorse for having put Vienne in danger, tries to commit suicide; but she prevents him, gives him a gold ring, and orders him to flee by himself, because her father will not kill her if he finds her alone.

Vienne throws herself on her father's mercy, who receives her back and decides to marry her to the son of the duke of Bourgoyne. Paris writes that he will go on pilgrimage and never see her more, but requests that she not take a husband. Vienne refuses to marry the son of the duke of Bourgoyne, so her father imprisons her with Isabel in an underground dungeon. The duke's son visits her to urge his suit, but she puts a chicken under her armpit so that it stinks, and he thinks she is rotting away from disease. Edward digs a tunnel to the dungeon and brings her food. Vienne wants to die.

Meanwhile, Paris sails to Venice and then to Alexandria, where he learns the language of the Moors and grows a beard. He travels in Moorish disguise to Jerusalem (via India and the land of Prester John) and then to Egypt, where he gains the favor of the sultan by curing his favorite falcon. At this time, the pope proclaims a crusade, and King Charles of France sends Vienne's father in disguise to spy upon the land. He is captured by agents of the sultan and imprisoned in Alexandria. The disguised Paris learns of his imprisonment, extracts from him the promise of any gift he may desire in return for his freedom, releases him by getting his jailers drunk, and returns with him to Vienne.

Vienne's father is willing to honor his promise, and Paris asks for the hand of his daughter, who is still in the dungeon. He visits her in his Moorish disguise, but she refuses him because she does not know who he is. The next day he returns with her ring, she recognizes him, and they are married. Edward marries Isabel, and they all live happily for forty years.

PARSON OF KALENBOROW.

The Parson of Kalenborow, Antwerp, J. van Doesborch, c. 1520. Ed. Edward Schröder, *Jahrbuch des Vereins für niederdeutsche Sprachforschung,* 13 (1887): 129–152. Anonymous translation of the Low German prose *Der Pfarrer von Kalenberg,* Lubeck, c. 1495, which is an adaptation of Philipp Frankfurter's early fifteenth-century German poem. About 10,000 words. A collection of some twenty independent jests illustrating the merry pranks of the parson of Kalenborow.

The church roof is in disrepair, so the parson gives his parishioners the choice of repairing the choir or the nave; they put a roof over the choir because that is cheaper, but when it rains the parson is dry and his parishioners are wet. The bishop orders the parson to discharge his young housekeeper and engage an older one aged over forty, so he hires two maids each aged twenty. The duke offers to pay for the repair of the parson's shoes, so he has them encased in silver. Etc.

PILGRIMAGE OF THE LIFE.

The Pilgrimage of the Lyfe of the Manhode. An anonymous prose translation, made in the early fifteenth century, of the first version of Guillaume de Deguileville's French verse *Le Pèlerinage de la vie humaine,* composed in 1330–31. About 73,000 words (including one poem). Six fifteenth-century MSS. Ed. William A. Wright, 1869 (Roxburghe Club), and Avril Henry, EETS 288, 1985, both from Cambridge University Library, MS Ff. 5. 30, the latter with full variants from all manuscripts. A whole-life allegory, told in the first person as a dream vision.

The author is reading the *Romance of the Rose,* when he falls asleep and dreams that he is a pilgrim seeking the Heavenly Jerusalem. On the way, he meets Grace Dieu, who instructs him in the dogmas of the church; he hears a lecture on transubstantiation, meets Penance and Charity, listens to Aristotle and Sapience, and is given armor which is too heavy for him. Grace Dieu leaves, and he meets Youth, who brings him to the Seven Deadly Sins, from whom he escapes by praying to the Virgin Mary. He meets Satan, from whom he escapes by swimming in the sea, and then he comes to an island where dwells the siren Worldly Pleasure. Next, Grace Dieu brings him to the castle of the Cistercians [Deguileville was a Cistercian monk], inhabited by Obedience, Abstinence, Chastity, and Poverty. The castle is stormed by Detraction, Treason, and Envy, but it stands fast. Then Infirmity and Age approach, and Grace warns him of the approach of Death. But just as he thinks that Death has seized him, he hears the "horologe of the convent that rang for the matins" and awakes "all sweatinge."

PILGRIMAGE OF THE SOUL.
The pylgremage of the sowle. W. Caxton, 1483; selections edited by Katherine I. Cust, 1859. An anonymous translation made in 1413 of Guillaume de Deguileville's French verse *Pèlerinage de l'ame*, composed in 1335. About 86,000 words (including 14 poems). Preserved in eight fifteenth-century MSS. An allegory of religious instruction, told in the first person in the form of a dream vision.

In the first of the five books into which the narrative is divided, the author dreams that he has died and sees Mercy bury his body and Prayer hasten before him to heaven. Satan claims him, but his Angel leads his Soul to judgment. He is taken to a trial at which even Reason pleads against the Soul, but Mercy gets a charter of pardon from heaven, and the Soul is sent to purgatory. The second book describes purgatory, explains the nature of pardon given by Holy Church, and reports a dialogue between the Body and the Soul. The third book describes the pains of hell. The fourth book returns to upper earth, where the author sees pilgrims playing between a green tree and a dry tree. The scheme of redemption is sketched. Here is inserted "a lytel declaracion of the nature of the sowle by addicion of the translatoure," and the book concludes with a description of an image in human shape made of many metals, which is compared to the body politic. In the fifth book, the author dreams that his Soul is taken from purgatory and led to the heavenly Jerusalem, where it receives instructions about the mansions of heaven. The work ends with songs by the angels (in verse) on the Nativity, Purification, Twelfth Day, and Easter.

PONTHUS.
The noble historye of Kynge Ponthus, W. de Worde, c. 1509, c. 1510, 1511, the fragment c. 1510 ed. Friedrich Brie, *Archiv,* 118 (1907); 325–328. For summary, see c. 1450 *Ponthus and Sidone,* below.

PONTHUS AND SIDONE.
King Ponthus and the Fair Sidone. An anonymous translation, c. 1450, of the French prose *Ponthus et la belle Sidoine,* c. 1390 (an adaptation, with considerable changes, of the Anglo-Norman poem *Horn et Rimenild,* c. 1170–80). About 45,000 words. Two MSS, ed. Frank J. Mather, Jr., *PMLA,* 12 (1897). A chivalric romance set at an indeterminate time in Spain, Brittany, and England; "a noble story, whereof a man may learn many good ensamples."

Brodas, son of the Sawdeyn of Babilon, invades Spain and kills King Tiber. The knight Patryk persuades the king's brother to save his life by pretending to be a Saracen, and he puts the king's son, Ponthus, and other children on a boat. The boat sails to Little Bretayn, where King Huguell rears Ponthus, and where his daughter, Sidone, falls in love with the boy. Ponthus is made a knight, battles the Saracens, and kills Carados, another son of the Sawdeyn. Guenelete, the envious companion of Ponthus, informs Sidone that Ponthus loves another. Ponthus, noticing her coolness, retires from court and, as the Black Knight, overcomes a warrior each week. At the end of the year, he is recognized and reconciled to Sidone.

Guenelete then tells the king that Ponthus loves his daughter dishonestly. Ponthus is banished and sails to England, where, under the name of La Surdyte, he is admired by the men and ladies of the English court. He captures the attacking king of Ireland and brings about peace between the two kings by suggesting that the king of Ireland marry the king of England's second daughter. He kills Corbatan, third son of the Sawdeyn. The king of England offers him his eldest daughter, but he refuses because he loves Sidone.

Sidone is to be married to the king of Burgoyne, but Ponthus returns to Little Bretayn, reveals himself to Sidone by means of a ring, and kills the king of Burgoyne in a joust. He says he will not marry Sidone until he has rid his own country of Saracens. He sails to Galice in Spain with an army where, with the help of the knight Patryk and his uncle (the earl of Destrue), he overcomes the Saracens and kills their leader, Brodas, son of the Sawdeyn.

Meanwhile, Guenelete forges letters saying that Ponthus, when dying, wished Sidone to marry him. Sidone "thought well that the letters were false," but in fear for the life of her father, she acquiesces. On the day set for the wedding, Ponthus returns, attends the feast as a dancer, and kills Guenelete. He marries Sidone, and his cousin Pollides marries Genever, daughter of the king of England. Ponthus gives advice on the proper conduct of a ruler and with Sidone lives long and generously as king of Little Bretayn.

REYNARD THE FOX.

The historye of reynart the foxe, W. Caxton, 1481, 1489, 1494, before 1506, c. 1525, 1550 (revised), and many later adaptations; ed. William J. Thoms, Percy Soc., 12 (1844); ed. W. F. Blake, EETSes 263, 1970. Translation by Caxton of the Dutch prose *Historie van Reinaert die Vos,* Gouda, 1479. About 43,000 words in forty-three chapters. The Dutch prose version that Caxton translated is a redaction of the Flemish metrical *Reinaerts Historie,* c. 1375, which derives from the French cycle *Roman de Renart,* begun about 1160, which in turn derives from the Latin poem *Ysengrimus,* c. 1150, by the Flemish poet Nivardus of Ghent, who gave the animals their now-familiar names.

The Lion, King of the Beasts, holds court, and the victims of Reynard the Fox complain. Bruin the Bear is sent to summon Reynard to court, but he is tricked and deprived of his ears. Reynard finally appears and is condemned to death; but he promises the Lion to reveal the location of a buried treasure, he is pardoned, and his accusers are made to suffer.

Reynard returns to his den at Maleperduis and arrogantly sends the head of Cuward the Hare back to court. He is again summoned to answer for his misdeeds, engages in a judicial combat with Isegrim the Wolf, and overcomes him by hitting below the belt. The Lion makes Reynard his favorite, and he returns home in glory.

ROBERT THE DEVIL.

The lyfe of Robert the Devyll, W. de Worde, c. 1500, c. 1517; ed. Henry Morley, *Early Prose Romances,* London, 1889. About 12,500 words. Anonymous translation of the French *La vie Robert le Diable,* Lyons, 1496. This work of religious propaganda, teaching that penitance will lead to salvation no matter how greatly one has sinned, was amazingly popular. The verse *Sir Gowther,* c. 1400, a metrical version of this prose tale, c. 1510, and Lodge's *Robert second duke of Normandy,* 1591, all tell the same story.

The duke and duchess of Normandy for a long time had no children, and the duchess vowed that if she had a child, she would give it to the Devil. Robert is born. Before he is a year old, he has teeth and mangles his wet nurse; later, he kills his schoolmaster and goes about robbing, murdering, and burning churches. His father sends men to capture him, and he puts out their eyes. He kills seven hermits and appears spattered with their blood before his mother. She tells him how she gave him to the Devil at his conception, and he vows to forsake the fiends and all their works.

Robert tells his band of thieves that he is going to repent; and when they refuse to leave thieving, he kills them all. He goes to Rome, where the pope sends him to a hermit to whom he confesses his sins. An angel instructs the hermit to prescribe for Robert as penance that he should pretend to be a fool, should eat with the dogs, and should not speak. The emperor's daughter is also mute. The seneschal, because the emperor will not give her to him, arranges for Saracens to besiege Rome. An angel gives Robert a white horse and armor, and on three successive occasions he defeats the Saracens. The emperor's daughter recognizes who he is, but cannot speak. The emperor, to find out who his champion is, sends men to waylay him, but he eludes them even though he is wounded in the thigh. The seneschal pretends to be the champion by stabbing himself in the thigh, and he claims the emperor's daughter. At the altar, the daughter regains her speech and says that the champion is the knight on the white horse. The angel informs Robert that he has completed his penance. He marries the emperor's daughter and returns with her to Rowane in Normandy.

SCOGGIN'S JESTS.

The First and best Part of Scoggins Jests: Full of witty mirth and pleasant shifts, done by him in France, and other places: being a preservation against Melancholy. Gathered by Andrew Boord, Doctor of Physicke, T. Colwell, c. 1570, 1626, c. 1680 (there were probably earlier now-lost editions); ed. W. C. Hazlitt, *Shakespeare Jest Books,* vol. 2, 1864. About 29,000 words in seventy-seven sections; composed before 1549.

A collection of anecdotes forming a jest-book biography of Tom Scoggin, a poor scholar who became an Oxford M. A., played many practical jokes, entered the service of Sir William Neville as a jester, was brought to the English court, offended the king, retired to Paris (where he was first favored and later banished by the French king), visited Cambridge, was finally pardoned by the English king, died of a cough, and at his own request was buried under the rainspout of Westminster Abbey where he would always have plenty to drink.

Many of the anecdotes are derivative (from as far back as Cicero's *De oratore,* to more recent collections such as *Salomon and Marcolphus,* 1492, and *A Hundred Mery Talys,* c. 1525), and some may have been invented by Borde, who probably created the character, for there is no good evidence of the historical existence of such a person. Bale, Shakespeare, and later writers confuse Borde's jester with John or Henry Scogan, a poet who was a contemporary of Chaucer.

SEVEN WISE MASTERS OF ROME.
Thystorye of the VII Wyse Maysters of Rome, R. Pynson, 1493, c. 1515, c. 1555, 1633, 1671 (abbreviated), etc.; ed. George Gomme, 1885 (Villon Society). A frame tale containing fifteen short stories.

Poncianus, the emperor of Rome, has a son, Dyoclesian, whom he puts under the charge of seven wise masters. When his first wife dies, the emperor marries a princess of Castille, who is jealous of his son. By magic, she arranges that if the son should speak within seven days, he would suffer great misfortune. The masters discover her plot and order him to remain silent for seven days. The empress accuses the son of attempting to rape her; the son remains silent, and the emperor orders him hanged. In the evening, the empress tells a story about the evil done by children; in the morning, the son is led to execution, but the masters tell a story of the evil done by women, and the execution is postponed until the following day (and so on through the seven days).

Fourteen stories are told: (Empress 1) an old tree is cut down because of the complaint of a young one; (Master 1) a serpent attacks a child, and a greyhound kills it, but it is killed by its master who thinks it has attacked the child; (E2) a shepherd by a trick kills a boar and marries the king's daughter; (M2) a husband locks out his wife, and she by a trick gets into the house and locks him out; (E3) a knight is caught stealing, and his son cuts off his head so he will not be recognized; (M3) a magpie who has been taught to speak tells a merchant of his wife's amours, but the wife by a trick causes the merchant to disbelieve the bird, which is then killed; (E4) seven wise masters cause an emperor to become blind; (M4) a wife tries the patience of her husband; (E5) four knights for the sake of gold destroy an image, given by Virgil, that protects the city; (M5) Galienus, a young physician, in envy kills his master, Ypocras; (E6) a steward sends his own wife to the king for money; (M6) a wife accepts money from three suitors, kills them, and by a ruse gets her brother to dispose of their bodies; (E7) a king locks his queen in a tower, a knight digs a tunnel and becomes her lover, and by passing back and forth they persuade the king that his queen is the knight's wife; (M7) a wife who mourns by her husband's grave becomes enamoured of the sheriff who is guarding the body of a criminal in the same cemetery (when the body of the criminal is stolen, she substitutes the body of her husband to save her new lover).

The seven days have now passed, so Dyoclesian tells a story of a dutiful son who was wrongly suspected by his father [this is the *Gesta Romanorum* friendship story of the two knights of Balduc]. He reveals the empress' false accusation, and she is burned at the stake. [There are two earlier Middle-English metrical versions of this frame tale, from the mid-fourteenth century, that contain a partly different set of stories.]

THREE KINGS' SONS.
The Three Kings' Sons, one MS, ed. F. J. Furnivall, EETSes 67, 1895. About 103,000 words. An anonymous translation made about 1500 of David Aubert's French prose *Trois fils de roi,* Lyons, 1501, composed in 1463.

Sicily is invaded by the Turks. Three princes—Philip of France, David of Scotland, and Humphrey of England—come incognito to help King Alfour of Sicily, and they all fall in love with his daughter, Iolante. Philip rescues King Alfour's general Ferant from the Turks and captures King Ferabras of Persia, whom he releases on his promise to aid Christians. David is shipwrecked, but he is rescued by the sultan's son, Orcays, who is later taken prisoner and also falls in love with Iolante. Humphrey, too, is shipwrecked, but he is saved by King Ferabras of Persia in accordance with the promise he had made to Philip. With the aid of the three princes, the sultan is slain, Sicily is freed from the Turks, and King Alfour is made emperor of Germany.

The three princes return to their own countries, find their fathers dead, and so become kings. The next year, they return to take part in a three-day tournament for the hand of the Princess Iolante. King Philip of France wins her; King Humphrey of England gives one of his sisters to King David of Scotland and another of his sisters to Sultan Orcays of Turkey, and he himself weds the sister of Sultan Orcays, since she and her brother have become Christians.

TROY.
The recuyell of the historyes of Troye, Bruges, W. Caxton, c. 1475 (the first book printed in English and, on the basis of number of editions, the most successful of Caxton's translations), reprinted 1502, [1503], 1553, 1596 (newly corrected by W. Fiston), 1607, 1617 (5th edition), 1636, 1663, 1670, 1676, 1680, 1684, 1702, 1708 (13th edition), 1738 (18th edition); 1802 (Roxburghe Club), [1810], 1892 (Kelmscott Press), 1894 (2 vols., Ed. H. O. Sommer, from c. 1475). Translation by Caxton, begun in 1471 and continued two years later, from Raoul Le Fèvre's *Le recueil des histoires de troies,* composed in 1464. About 210,000 words.

Book I. The main stories of early Greek mythology: the wars between Uranus, his sons Titan and Saturn, and Saturn's son Jupiter; the amours of Jupiter with Calisto, Danes, and Alcumena; Perseus beheads Meduse and rescues Andromeda from the sea monster; the birth of Hercules; he rescues Laomedon's daughter Exiona; Laomedon shuts him out of Troy, and he destroys the city.

Book II. The later life of Hercules: he kills the lions of Nemee, Busire, and the Centaures; rescues Proserpyne from hell; loves Megera and kills her in a fit of jealousy; kills Laomedon and destroys Troy a second time; loves Deyanira; overcomes Achelous, Nessus, the serpent of Lerne, Gerion, Cacus, and Pryscus; falls in love with Yole; overcomes Dyomedes; receives the poisoned shirt of Nessus from Deyanira and dies.

Book III. The final fall of Troy: Priamus rebuilds the city; his son Parys abducts Melayne; the Greeks sail for Troy, and the Trojan Calcas joins them; various battles follow—in the sixth, Dyomedes gets Troylus' horse and sends it to Calcas' daughter, Breseyda; in the eighth, Achilles treacherously kills Hector. Achilles falls in love with Polixene, sister of Hector, and for a time refuses to fight against the Trojans; the Greeks retire to their ships; Achilles re-enters the battle and kills the unarmed Troylus; Parys ambushes and kills Achilles; Parys and Ajax kill one another. Eneas and Anthenor give the Palladyum to Ulixes. By means of a horse of brass, built as a result of the advice of Calcas, Troy is destroyed for the third time. The Greeks spare the traitors, Anthenor and Eneas.

VALENTINE AND ORSON.

The Hystory of the two valyaunte brethren Valentyne and Orson, sonnes unto the Emperour of Grece, W. de Worde, c. 1510, c. 1555, c. 1565, c. 1565, 1637; ed. Arthur Dickson, EETSes 204, 1937. About 130,000 words. Translation by Henry Watson of the French prose *Valentin et Orson*, Lyon, 1489, based on a lost fourteenth-century French poem. A chivalric romance loosely connected with the Charlemagne cycle.

Bellysant, sister of King Pepyn of France, marries Alexander, emperor of Constantinople. The archbishop of Constantinople loves her, but she rejects his advances, so he slanders her to the emperor, who banishes her with her squire, Blandymain. She returns to France, and in a forest near Orleans gives birth to twins, one of whom is carried off by a bear. The second child is found by King Pepyn, who names him Valentine and educates him at court. The bear nurses the first child, Orson, who grows up among beasts for fifteeen years and does not learn to speak. Meanwhile, Bellysant and Blandymain wander to Portugal, where the giant Ferragus befriends them.

Valentine distinguishes himself by raising the siege of Rome, and Pepyn makes him an earl, which causes the king's illegitimate sons, Haufray and Henry, to be jealous. Pepyn offers a reward for the capture of Orson, the wild man who terrifies the country people. Valentine fights Orson, who finally yields and comes to court, where he is baptized. The duke of Aquitaine asks for aid against the Greene Knight, brother of Ferragus, who can only be overcome by a king's son who had never nursed at the breasts of a woman. Valentine and Orson go to Aquitaine, where the duke's daughter, Fezon, falls in love with Orson. Valentine fights the Greene Knight to a draw, but the next day Orson overcomes him, though he spares his life at the intercession of Valentine. The Greene Knight invites the brothers to visit his sister, Clerimond, who owns a Brazen Head that can talk.

Meanwhile, Blandymain tells Pepyn of Bellysant's two children, and he deduces that they are Valentine and Orson. He goes to Constantinople to tell their father, the emperor, who is besieged by Saracens. The two brothers are received by Clerimond, who falls in love with Valentine. The Brazen Head informs them that they are brothers, and it tells how Orson can be given the power of speech by cutting a thread under his tongue. Valentine is affi-anced to Clerimond after she agrees to become a Christian. Her dwarf, the enchanter Pacolet (who has a wooden horse that sails through the air), flies to her brother Ferragus in Por-tugal and tells him that she is about to marry a Christian. To prevent this, Ferragus cap-tures Valentine and Orson and imprisons them in Portugal; but Pacolet frees them by magic and brings them to Aquitaine on his wooden horse, where Orson marries Fezon. Pacolet then transports Valentine and the Greene Knight to Constantinople, where they defeat the Saracens; Bellysant arrives by ship and is reconciled to her husband, the emperor.

Meanwhile, a Saracen named Trompart steals Pacolet's horse and carries Clerimond to India, where the king falls in love with her. Valentine and Pacolet go in search of her, finally reach India, and carry her off on Pacolet's horse. Valentine then marries Clerimond. Later, Valentine is besieged by Saracens; his father, the emperor of Constantinople, comes to rescue him, and in order to reach him disguises himself in pagan garments; Valentine thinks he is a Saracen and kills him. When he realizes his error, he almost goes mad.

Meanwhile at Paris, Haufray and Henry, Pepyn's illegitimate sons, poison him and his queen, but they cannot find the legitimate heir, Charlemagne, to do away with him. With the help of the king of England, they are slain and Charlemagne is crowned.

Valentine and Orson are chosen joint emperors of Constantinople, but Valentine is so overcome by grief at having killed his father that he leaves his wife, Clerimond, and goes to Rome, where he confesses his sins to a hermit. The hermit enjoins him as penance to return to his palace, reveal his identity to no one, never speak, sleep under the stairs, and feed only on scraps thrown to the dogs for seven years. At the end of the seven years, he reveals himself by letter to Clerimond and dies. She grieves and lives alone thereafter. Orson reigns seven years, then retires to the woods and lives upon roots. After his death, his children succeed him as emperor and are instructed in ruling by the Greene Knight.

VIRGILIUS.
The lyfe of Virgilius and of his deth and many marvayles that he dyd in his lyfe tyme by whychcraft and nygramansy thorowgh the helpe of the devyls of hell, Antwerp, J. van Does-boroch, c. 1518, London, c. 1550. About 10,500 words in 22 chapters. Ed. Henry Morley, *Early Prose Romances,* 1889. An anonymous translation of the Dutch *Virgilius Van zijn leven, doct, ende vanden wonderlijcken wercken die hi dede by nigromancien,* Antwerp, c. 1512, with some consultation of a French version. The Dutch is a free adaptation, with some omissions and four added episodes, of the French *Les faictz merveilleux de Virgille,* Paris, c. 1511, which in turn was compiled from various medieval sources (see John W. Spargo, *Virgil the Necromancer,* Cambridge, Mass., 1934, 236–253). It is a birth-to-death life of Virgil the magician, who is unrelated to Virgil the poet.

Remus, the son of Remus, has a son, Virgilius. Virgilius frees a devil from a hole covered by a board, and he in gratitude teaches him magic. Virgilius asks him how he could get out of so small a hole; the devil shows him by crawling into the hole, and Virgilius covers it again with the board. He loves a lady of Rome who lives in a high tower; she lets down a basket on a rope so he can climb into it and visit her, but she pulls it only halfway up and leaves him dangling for all to see. In revenge, he puts out all the fires in Rome and provides that they can only be rekindled at her buttocks. He constructs an image that when looked at quenches sexual desire; his wife angrily casts it down. He makes a metal serpent which has the property that whoever puts his hand into its mouth can only pull it out if he tells the truth. A man who suspects his wife of infidelity has her put her hand in the serpent's mouth; she dresses her lover as a fool, and when her husband asks about her lover, she replies that she has no more to do with him than with the fool standing by. Virgilius finally dies in an attempt to restore his youth.

This is really a jest book—a series of anecdotes whose only connection is that they all concern a man named Virgilius.

WILLIAM OF PALERMO.
Kyng Wyllyam of Palerne. Printed by Wynkyn de Worde, c. 1515 (only a two-leaf fragment survives, ed. Friedrich Brie, *Archiv*, 118 [1907]: 318–325). Anonymous translation and adaptation, c. 1515, of a derivative of the Old French metrical *Guillaume de Palerne*, c. 1195 (a derivative different from the French prose version by Pierre Durand printed at Lyons in 1552). Probably about 20,000 words. A chivalric romance concerning a werewolf. The following summary is reconstructed from the Middle English alliterative version of c. 1375.

The king of Apulia has a son named William and a daughter named Florence. His brother, wishing to inherit the throne, bribes two ladies to murder William, but as the child plays at Palerne (Palermo), a wolf runs off with him and carries him to a forest near Rome. The wolf is Prince Alphouns of Spain, who has been enchanted by his stepmother, Queen Braunde, in order that her son, Braundinis, may inherit the throne.

The emperor of Rome finds William and gives him to his daughter, Melior, as a page. Melior falls in love with William and he with her. The emperor of Greece proposes that his son marry Melior, to which her father accedes. With the help of Melior's friend Alisaundrine, the lovers dress in the skins of two white bears and flee from Rome. They are cared for by the werewolf and at last come to Palermo. There they find that William's father is dead and the city is being besieged by the king of Spain, who demands the hand of William's sister, Florence, for his son, Braundinis.

William leads the defenders of Palermo and takes the king of Spain and his son, Braundinis, prisoner. He then demands that the werewolf be disenchanted. Queen Braunde restores Alphouns to his proper shape and is given a pardon; William marries Melior; the former werewolf, Alphouns, marries William's sister, Florence; and Alphouns' half-brother, Braundinis, marries Melior's confidante, Alisaundrine.

WONDERFUL NEWS.
Wonderfull newes of the death of Paule the .iii. last byshop of Rome, and of diverse thynges that after his death have happened, where in is truly set out the abhominable actes of his most mischevous life: Written in Latin by P. Esquillus, and Englyshed by W[illiam] B[aldwin], *Londoner*, T. Gaultier, c. 1552. About 10,000 words. That Baldwin was the translator is indicated by the combination of his initials and his personal motto, "Love and Live," in the preface. This is a translation of *Epistola de Morte Pauli Tertii Pontificis Maximis de que iis quae ei post mortem eius acciderunt*, Piacenza [for Basel?], 1549, sometimes attributed to Pietro Paolo Vergerio, a former Italian bishop who had joined the Protestant reformers. It is a letter purportedly written from Rome on 11 November 1549 (the day after the death of Pope Paul III) by P. Aesquillus to his friend Mar[cus] Forius (i.e. Pasquillus and Marforius,

statues so named located at opposite sides of Rome on which satires and lampoons were often posted).

The letter is in the first person: When Pope Paul III dies, my Genius brings me to the pope's palace, where I see Dracolicus carry him to hell. We see him change into a foul hag, clothed in a dress on which are figured his most notable crimes, and sit on a spotted beast with seven heads and ten horns. His son, Peter Aloysius, meets him and berates him for having said there was no hell, so that he had thought he could commit crimes without punishment. We follow Paul III to the city of Pluto, where his crimes are engraved on pillars of adamant: he forced his sister to become the mistress of Alexander Borgia and poisoned his mother; after he was made a cardinal, he begot a son; when he became pope, he committed incest with his daughter Constance; he overcame the Perusines and drove Ascanius Colona from his kingdom; he gave Parma and Placencia to his son; he cast horoscopes and gave bribes; he led the forces of the church against Christians and desired to "swim in the blood of Lutherans."

Genius then shows me the feast prepared by Pluto at which the kings of the earth engendered with the whore with the golden cup, after which they were thrown into a pond of brimstone to be punished forever. "This is the end of the great Bishop Paul." Then Genius leads me back to earth, as before us was led the seven-headed beast with the cup on its back—gifts which Pluto was sending to Paul's successor. So we return to Rome, and I write this to you, my Forius. Halcyon days will come again. Adieu.

XENOPHON.
The Bookes of Xenophon Contayning the discipline, schole, and education of Cyrus the noble Kyng of Persie. Translated out of Greeke into Englysshe, by Master Wylliam Barkar. Printed by R. Wolfe, c. 1552 (books 1–6 only), 1567 (all eight books); c. 114,000 words.

A pseudo-biography, written in the fourth century B.C., of Cyrus the Great, founder of the Achaemenid Persian Empire (he reigned 559–529 B.C.). Cyrus is portrayed as an irresistible conqueror and an ideal ruler who became so through qualities of mind and character that were formed by his education, first at the Persian court of his father, Cambyses, and afterwards at the court of his maternal grandfather, Astyages, King of Media. In early manhood, he aids his uncle Cyaxares, who had succeeded as king of Media, against the Assyrians. By kind and generous treatment, he persuades Armenians, Hyrcanians, and other enemies to join him—especially the Assyrians Gobryas and Gadatas, who had been wronged by their king.

At a division of spoils, Cyrus is allotted Panthea of Susa, reputed to be the most beautiful woman in Asia. He puts her under the care of his friend Araspas, who boasts he can control his affections but falls overwhelmingly in love with her. Cyrus sends Araspas away to spy on Croesus, king of Lydia, and at the intercession of Panthea he receives her husband, Abradatas, into his service. A detailed description follows of Panthea's reunion with her husband and of her arming him on the eve of the battle against Croesus. Abradatas is assigned by lot to the forward position and is killed in the first charge. Panthea stabs herself and dies near the corpse of her husband. This is the earliest romantic love story in extant prose literature, and Panthea was the first heroine to die for love (though after Virgil's Dido there were many).

Cyrus defeats Croesus, takes him prisoner, but treats him kindly. He then marches on Babylon, which he captures by surprise. He reorganizes the government of his dominion, which extends from Syria to Egypt. Finally, he is warned in a dream to prepare for death, makes a farewell speech to his children and friends, and leaves the throne to his eldest son, Cambyses.